Rowe v. Pacific Quad, Inc.

Fifth Edition

Deposition Materials
Plaintiff

Rowe v. Pacific Quad, Inc.

Fifth Edition

Deposition Materials
Plaintiff

Fred C. Moss

S.M.U. Dedman School of Law
Dallas, Texas

David Benjamin Oppenheimer

UC Berkeley School of Law
Berkeley, CA

NITA

National Institute for Trial Advocacy

Address inquiries to:

Reprint Permission
National Institute for Trial Advocacy
1685 38th Street, Suite 200
Boulder, CO 80301-2735
Phone: (800) 225-6482
Fax: (720) 890-7069
E-mail: permissions@nita.org

ISBN 978-1-60156-347-7
FBA 1347

14 13 12 11 10 9 8 7 6 5 4 3 2 1
Printed in the United States of America

Wolters Kluwer

Official co-publisher of NITA.
WKLegaledu.com/NITA

Preface to the Fifth Edition

Rowe v. Pacific Quad was first published by NITA as a trial file in 1986. It was written by David Oppenheimer, then the director of the Boalt Hall Employment Discrimination Clinic, with substantial collaboration from Ignatius Bau, for use in the clinic's trial advocacy course. Fred Moss adapted the file for use in deposition courses in 2000. In the years that followed, three new editions of each file were published. Each edition brought more differences between the trial file and deposition file.

We co-authored this fifth edition of both files to bring them back together. Students and practicing lawyers using the files will find that the facts and law are now entirely consistent within the two files.

The case is set in Nita City, in the State of Nita, and is to be litigated and tried in the Superior Court of the County of Darrow. California substantive law is generally used, and virtually all of the citations to Nita statutes and cases in turn correspond to citations in the various California codes and cases in the California Reports and California Appellate Reports. The procedural aspects of the case, however, use federal law.

Though written before the Anita Hill hearings, the 1991 Civil Rights Act, and all but one of the Supreme Court's five major decisions on sexual harassment law, the *Rowe* case file has held up remarkably well. Those who have used the first, second, third, or fourth editions will find most of the basic facts unchanged, but some fine-tuning of the materials gives it a twenty-first century feel, plus a substantial re-writing of the legal memo (in the form of an appellate decision) brings the file into conformity with Title VII and California FEHA law.

We are grateful to the many people who helped us draft and improve the file over the years, including Denise Abrams, Mark Caldwell, Jeffrey B. Demain, Anne Kamsvaag, Sam Miller, Lois Schwartz, Julie Ann Talbo, and Courtney Whang. They deserve substantial credit for its success. Its limitations and liabilities, however, are entirely our responsibility.

Fred C. Moss
S.M.U. Dedman School of Law
Dallas, Texas

David B. Oppenheimer
Berkeley Law
Berkeley, California

Contents

INTRODUCTION

The plaintiff, Alice Rowe, has brought an action for sexual harassment and wrongful discharge against her employer, Pacific Quad, Inc. Ms. Rowe had worked for Pacific Quad for less than two weeks before walking off the job. She asserts that her supervisor, operations manager Stanley Schmit, continually leered at her, made offensive sexually suggestive comments to her, brushed by her in order to sexually touch her, and, finally, propositioned her. She further alleges that the president of Pacific Quad, John Walsh, was informed of the harassment and ratified it. Rowe had previously filed a sexual harassment claim, which was dismissed, against a professor when she was in college.

The defendant, Pacific Quad, denies that the harassment occurred. Pacific Quad is a small (twelve employees) high-tech company that designs software packages for medium-sized companies to help them improve the efficiency of their computer operations. Walsh and Schmit claim that Rowe was a highly nervous, marginally productive administrative assistant who was likely to be dismissed the week after she walked off the job. They claim to be mystified as to why she quit but speculate that she was paranoid or was extremely oversensitive and misunderstood the friendly atmosphere of their small, family-like office.

Rowe claims lost wages, medical expenses (psychotherapy), general damages for emotional distress, and punitive damages.

The applicable law is found in the appellate decision reversing dismissal of the case.

All years in these materials are identified in the following form:

YR-0 indicates the actual year in which the case is being tried (that is, the present year);
YR-1 indicates the first year preceding;
YR-2 indicates the second year preceding, etc.

Counsel and witnesses should calculate the specific year indicated by the "YR minus [X]" device in the file and use the actual year when referring to dates. For example, the year "YR-1" is last year (the current year minus one), and "YR-2" is two years ago. In short, assuming it is now 2013, rather than saying "year one" or "year minus one" for "YR-1," say "2012."

ELECTRONIC EXHIBITS

Electronic versions of the exhibits are available for download here:
http://bit.ly/1P20Jea

Password: Rowe5plaintiff

Materials Available to All Sides

Special Instructions for Use as a Deposition Program File

Issues

The witnesses in this case file may be deposed on the issue of liability only, or on both the issues of liability and damages. Counsel will receive instruction on this point from the program faculty.

Witnesses

The following witnesses may be deposed by the parties:

By the plaintiff:

John Walsh
Stanley Schmit
Susan Robinson

By the defendant:

Alice Rowe
Gloria Warner
Anna Mills

Stipulated Facts

1. The records of the Nita Department of Fair Employment and Housing were supplied to the parties by the Nita Department of Fair Employment and Housing pursuant to the Nita Public Records Act.

2. The résumés (PQ-0007 – PQ-00019) were produced by Pacific Quad in response to a discovery request.

3. In YR-1, January 29 was a Friday, February 1 was a Monday, and February 12 was a Friday.

4. Annie Cunningham is unavailable as a witness. Her notes (DFEH-0010 – DFEH-0015) and the emails (DFEH-0016 – DFEH-0020) in the Nita Department of Fair Employment and Housing documents were produced pursuant to the Nita Public Records Act.

5. The parties stipulate to the following timeline.

February 1, YR-1	Alice Rowe begins work at Pacific Quad
February 12, YR-1	Alice Rowe's employment at Pacific Quad ends
March 23, YR-1	Alice Rowe files administrative complaint with DFEH

March 23 – September 17, YR-1	DFEH investigation period
September 20, YR-1	Alice Rowe files Complaint in Superior Court
October 5, YR-1	Pacific Quad moves to dismiss
October 15, YR-1	Motion to Dismiss granted
November 15, YR-1	Final Order of Dismissal
December 15, YR-1	Appeal filed, argued, and submitted
December 30, YR-1	Appeal decided
January 15, YR-0	Answer filed
January 25, YR-0	Discovery documents exchanged

IN THE SUPERIOR COURT
OF DARROW COUNTY,
NITA CIVIL DIVISION

ALICE ROWE,	)	
	)	
Plaintiff	)	
	)	
v.	)	Civ. No. 0-9876543
	)	
PACIFIC QUAD, INC.,	)	COMPLAINT
	)	
Defendant.		

COMES NOW Plaintiff ALICE ROWE, a resident and citizen of Nita City, State of Nita, complaining of Defendant PACIFIC QUAD, INC., a corporation duly incorporated and existing under and by virtue of the law of the State of Nita, with its domicile and principal place of business in the City of Nita, Darrow County, State of Nita, and alleges as follows:

1. Stanley Schmit (hereinafter referred to as "Schmit") is, and at all times relevant to this action has been, employed by PACIFIC QUAD, INC., (hereinafter referred to as "PACIFIC QUAD" or "Defendant") in the capacity of operations manager.
2. On or about January 29, YR-1, Plaintiff applied for the position of administrative assistant at PACIFIC QUAD. Schmit interviewed Plaintiff, informed her that she had been hired, and told her to report to work on the following Monday, February 1, YR-1.
3. Plaintiff reported to work at PACIFIC QUAD on February 1, YR-1, and worked there until the middle of the day on February 12, YR-1.
4. During the interview on January 29, YR-1, and throughout the two weeks that Plaintiff worked at PACIFIC QUAD, Plaintiff's immediate supervisor, operations manager Schmit, subjected Plaintiff to repeated verbal sexual harassment, including, but not limited to, comments directed at various parts of both Plaintiff's and Schmit's anatomy.
5. Throughout the two weeks that Plaintiff worked at PACIFIC QUAD, Schmit subjected Plaintiff to repeated physical sexual harassment, including, but not limited to, unwanted and unsolicited touching.
6. During the interview on January 29, YR-1, and throughout the two weeks that Plaintiff worked at PACIFIC QUAD, Schmit subjected Plaintiff to repeated visual sexual harassment, including, but not limited to, leers of a sexual nature.
7. On or about February 12, YR-1, operations manager Schmit made an unsolicited and unwanted sexual advance toward Plaintiff. Plaintiff rejected Schmit's proposition.
8. On or about the same day, February 12, YR-1, both Schmit and Schmit's supervisor, the president of PACIFIC QUAD, John Walsh, conditioned Plaintiff's continued employment

upon her toleration of Schmit's verbal and physical sexual harassment and upon her consenting to Schmit's sexual demands. Walsh further informed Plaintiff that she could "leave" if she was not "happy" with her job. Thus, Walsh made accession to Schmit's sexual demands an implied condition of Plaintiff's employment.

9. On or about February 12, YR-1, Plaintiff was constructively terminated by Defendant in retaliation for her refusal to consent to operations manager Schmit's sexual demands.

10. Defendant's treatment of Plaintiff constitutes sexual harassment in employment, an unlawful employment practice in violation of the Fair Employment and Housing Act of the State of Nita, Nita Government Code Section 12940(i).

11. Defendant's termination of Plaintiff constitutes sexual harassment in employment, an unlawful employment practice in violation of the Fair Employment and Housing Act of the State of Nita, Nita Government Code Section 12940(i).

12. Defendant's conduct in harassing and terminating Plaintiff was oppressive and malicious, and was carried out by a managing agent of the corporation.

13. On or about March 23, YR-1, Plaintiff filed a verified complaint with the Department of Fair Employment and Housing of the State of Nita ("DFEH") alleging that she had been sexually harassed and terminated by Defendant PACIFIC QUAD.

14. On or about September 10, YR-1, Plaintiff received from the DFEH a notice of her right to bring suit in this action.

15. As a result of Defendant's unlawful employment practices, Plaintiff has suffered lost wages and employment benefits in an amount that has not yet been determined, but which exceeds the jurisdictional limit of this court.

16. As a result of Defendant's unlawful employment practices, Plaintiff has incurred expenses for personal and career counseling in an amount that has not yet been determined, but which exceeds the jurisdictional limit of this court.

17. As a result of Defendant's unlawful employment practices, Plaintiff has suffered humiliation, embarrassment, and severe emotional stress.

18. As a result of Defendant's unlawful employment practices, Plaintiff has suffered from insomnia, depression, and nightmares.

WHEREFORE Plaintiff prays judgment against Defendant:

1) For back pay in an amount to be determined at trial;
2) For special damages in an amount to be determined at trial;
3) For general damages in an amount to be determined at trial;
4) For exemplary damages in an amount to be determined at trial; and
5) For such other and further relief as may seem proper to this Court.

DATE: September 20, YR-1

Respectfully submitted,

Benjamin J. Cohen
Attorney for Plaintiff
1341 Haven Court
Nita City, Nita 99990
(721) 555-0479

Return of Summons

I hereby certify that the above Complaint and Summons were personally served on Henry Glenn on the 21st day of September YR-1.

Process Server

IN THE SUPERIOR COURT
OF DARROW COUNTY,
NITA CIVIL DIVISION

ALICE ROWE,	)	
	)	
Plaintiff	)	
	)	
v.	)	Civ. No. O-9876543
	)	
	)	
	)	
PACIFIC QUAD, INC.,	)	ANSWER
	)	
Defendant.	)	

Defendant for its answer to the complaint on file herein, admits and denies as follows:

1. Defendant admits the allegations contained in the following paragraphs of Plaintiff's complaint, which are numbered 1, 2, and 3.
2. Defendant denies each and every allegation contained in the following paragraphs of Plaintiff's complaint, which are numbered 4, 5, 6, 7, 8, 9, 10, 11, 15, 16, 17, and 18.
3. Defendant has insufficient knowledge or information to form a belief as to the truth of the allegations set forth in the paragraphs numbered 12, 13, and 14 of Plaintiff's complaint, and on that basis denies the allegations.

WHEREFORE, Defendant prays that Plaintiff take nothing by her said complaint.

DATE: January 15, YR-0

Henry Glenn

Henry Glenn
Attorney for Defendant
Glenn & O'Malley
100 Zee Street, Suite 801
Nita City, Nita 99990 (721) 555-1771

Certificate of Service

I hereby certify that on January 15, YR-0, a copy of the above Answer was placed in the United States mail, postage prepaid, addressed to Benjamin Cohen, 1341 Haven Court, Nita City, Nita 99990.

Barbara Phillips

Barbara Phillips
Glenn & O'Malley
100 Zee Street, Suite 801
Nita City, Nita 99990

Materials Available Only to the Plaintiff's Attorneys

Statement of Alice Rowe

Background

My name is Alice Rowe. I live at 1040 Redwood Lane, Nita City, Nita. I have lived in Nita City my whole life. I am twenty-seven years old. I am single and live with my parents in our family home. I am the youngest of three sisters. My sisters, Mary and Elizabeth, are married and live in other states with their husbands and families. Mary is a nurse, and Elizabeth owns a gift shop.

I grew up in a middle-class family. My mother did not work outside the home. My father was a small building contractor and a deacon in our church. He built everything from homes and barns to churches and strip malls. He is disabled and retired now. I am the first person in my family to attend college. I know it's supposed to be good thing, but sometimes it's hard for me knowing that my parents would prefer that I settle down instead. I'd like to settle down too. It probably doesn't help that I get really nervous every time I meet a new guy who I think I like. I have dated since junior year in high school. I don't have a steady boyfriend now, but I've started dating a nice guy I met at church. We'll see how it goes.

I guess I would describe myself as a quiet person; some would say I'm shy. I've never had lots of friends, just one or two close ones—mainly girls in our church. After I graduated from high school, I started going to Nita State University. That was in the fall of YR-9. I didn't make too many new friends when I started at Nita State either. I got along with all of my classmates, but I didn't participate in many of the social activities. I did volunteer to work with the Nita State Women's Association, where I served as secretary for one year.

After three semesters, I think it was, I took some time off from school and got a job as a secretary at a trucking company, Dodd's Trucking, starting in January YR-7. My boss was Mr. Don Dodd. It was a small, family-run company that did local hauling.

I left school partly because I needed the money and partly because I didn't know what I wanted to major in, or anything, so it seemed like a good idea to do something else for a while. I was feeling a little guilty, attending classes but not really pursuing any particular career. My parents would constantly ask me when I would be done with college, and I figured I would just take time off until I could figure out a solid plan.

The first job at Dodd's lasted for about six months until sometime in July YR-7. I left Dodd's because I got a better paying job as a secretary at Flash Computers. I was ready to leave Dodd's because some of the truckers working there were pretty crude. They used profanity and told dirty jokes all of the time. There were calendars in the office with nude women on them. One truck driver kept after me the whole time I was there, leering, asking me out, finding excuses to put his arm around me, and telling me I had a "nice body." I never told Mr. Dodd or anyone about what happened or how I felt there, but I was happy to leave.

At Flash Computers, my boss was Max Rexroth. It was a very small company that assembled desktop computers for individuals and small businesses to meet custom specifications. I didn't have any problems there like I had at Dodd's, but after a couple of months, I thought I should try to take some classes about computers, because it seemed like an interesting subject.

I saved enough to go back to school at Nita State in the spring of YR-6. Things went better that semester. I was learning to concentrate on my studies. I took some computer classes and did pretty well in them. I intended to graduate with a bachelor of science in computer science. This would require me to take courses such as Principles of Computer Science (an overview course), Data Structures and Database Management, Program Languages (such as HTML5, C, C++, C#, Java, JavaScript, Perl, Python, Ruby, Shell, SQL and Visual Basic), and Operating Systems and Systems Software (like the UNIX operating system for mainframe computers and PC-based operating systems such as Windows, Linux, and OS-X). I didn't want to become a software engineer, but I wanted to be more than a secretary, and I felt like computers was the right field to be in. That summer, I took a couple of courses and worked part time at the university's cafeteria.

The fall of YR-6 wasn't as good, though. I ended up with very boring classes, and I was running out of money again, so in January YR-5, I got another job as a secretary in a computer software company, GAM Software, working for a Mr. Bridge. I had no problems with anyone there. They treated me well.

I stayed at that job until August YR-5, but then I got laid off because the company was losing money. It was too late then to go back to school for that semester, so I got another secretary job at Nita Marine Insurance Company, which I kept until July YR-4. My supervisor was a Mr. Pico. Again, I had no problems with anyone there.

By then, I was determined to go back to school to finish my degree. I needed four more semesters of work to earn a bachelor of science degree in computer science.

The complaint against Professor Melvyl

That fall semester in YR-4 started off pretty well, but I had problems in one of my classes. I filed a complaint against Professor James Melvyl. I was taking his American History Through Literature seminar. I noticed that the Professor Melvyl kept staring at me. He made lots of sexual comments—jokes that obviously had some sexual double meaning from the way that he and some of the students laughed at them. He always looked at me when he made the jokes. I felt embarrassed, humiliated, degraded, and angry. I think the other students realized what was going on before I did.

At first, I just tried to ignore him, but then I had a meeting with him in his office to discuss the paper I was writing. It's so long ago now that I don't really remember the details of what happened, but I remember that he asked me to go out with him. I told him that I would not, and then told him how very unhappy I was about his constant use of sexual innuendos in class and the way he looked at me when he said those things. I may have started to cry. He put his arm around me, and claimed I misunderstood him. I screamed, "Don't," and ran out of his office. When I tried to talk to him about it later, he pretended that he didn't know what I was talking about. After that, he ignored me in class, so finally I decided to file a complaint against him. By then, I was so upset that I had pretty much stopped going to his class.

The school had a grievance board for sexual harassment complaints, and there was a hearing on my complaint. Of course, the professor denied everything, and because it was only my word against his, the complaint was dismissed. But I felt vindicated by the grievance board. As I said, everyone realized what was really going on. The hearing was very embarrassing for the professor, and I'm sure that he never again treated anyone else that way. I've never had the same kind of problem with any of my other professors, nor did I have any problems with my high school teachers.

Anna Mills

At some point, during this problem with Professor Melvyl in the fall of YR-4, someone suggested that I go see a counselor at the Women's Center at Nita State because I was very upset by it. That was when I started seeing Anna Mills, a counselor there. She helped me file my complaint. I continued my counseling sessions with Anna when I was out of school, too. I saw her regularly—about once a week—until around mid-YR-2. I was doing very well at that time and stopped seeing her altogether. My visits to her in the year preceding that time had dropped off to once a month. We agreed around May YR-2 that I should visit for further counseling only if and when I felt the need. So, at the time I applied for the job at Pacific Quad, I was not seeing Anna at all. However, after my run-in with Schmit, I started seeing Anna again, two to three times a week.

Anna has helped me understand that I have a poor self-image—"low self-esteem" she calls it. She says that I'm very bright and I'm torn between my belief that I could be a success working outside the home and my upbringing where I learned I should want to be a good wife, mother, and homemaker. This leads to what she calls my "fear of success."

Anna has made me realize that I would be happier and more productive if I stopped feeling guilty for wanting to have a career. She's also made me realize that my low self-esteem is part of what makes me nervous around my peers, especially the ones that are different from me. She explained that when I have better self-esteem, I will be more comfortable around people who are different than me and more comfortable when people give me praise or attention. That is what we're working on.

Anna really helped me without being judgmental—never disbelieving me or implying that I was crazy. She has never doubted that Professor Melvyl or Stan Schmit did what I said they did. She's accepted it and helped me develop a tougher skin. Between the time of the Professor Melvyl incident and when I began working at Pacific Quad, I had really embraced my decision to seek a career and was optimistically moving ahead toward a bright future. I was really feeling and doing great. My visits to Anna had ceased altogether. Then, the encounter with Schmit really shook my confidence. I wasn't sure anymore if I could handle working if people were going to treat me that way. I was in worse shape than when I was abused by Professor Melvyl.

When I was a student, I was not charged for the counseling. I would go once a week. When I was not in school, I continued seeing Anna every two weeks or so, and paid her $65 per session. After I quit my job at Pacific Quad, I started seeing Anna two to three times a week. I've probably seen her about 100 times since February YR-1 and paid her over $8,000. I'm not sure exactly how much. Currently, for the past month, I've been seeing her only once a week.

I finished out the semester that was marred by Professor Melvyl's outrageous conduct, and I decided to get a job again. I worked as a secretary at Starbuck Software from January YR-3 through August YR-3. I went back to school, and had a good semester that fall.

I had been working as a secretary during the spring and summer of YR-2, and I had completed the fall semester of YR-2 at school when I applied for the job at Pacific Quad. I would have liked to have stayed at school and finished my degree in the spring of YR-1, but I went to work instead because I needed the money.

Pacific Quad

I saw an ad on Craigslist for the administrative assistant's job at Pacific Quad at the beginning of the week before I actually started working there. I think that was on Tuesday. I called, and they told me to come in and fill out an application. I went in that same afternoon. One of the secretaries gave me an application form to fill out—the standard questions about skills, experience, education. I didn't talk to anyone else there that day. Somebody called me the next day—I think it was the same secretary—and we arranged for me to come in for an interview on Friday, January 29, YR-1.

The interview took place in Mr. Schmit's office. I was alone with him with the door shut. I was a little nervous at first. I'd had a lot of expenses recently—my car died, and I was trying to pay Anna Mills what I still owed her—and I knew that I had to find a job pretty soon. Besides, I think people are always a little nervous in interviews.

At first, the interview seemed pretty run-of-the-mill. He asked me the usual questions about my prior jobs and talked about what they were looking for. After a couple of minutes, though, the way he was looking at me started to make me feel uncomfortable. He wasn't exactly staring at me, but he was looking at my breasts and not at my face when he spoke to me. After a few minutes, he got up, and came around to the side of the desk where I was sitting. We kept talking, mostly about computers, while he paced around, not too far from me. Then he told me that he liked me, and would call me later that afternoon about the job. He called me in the middle of the afternoon and offered me the job. He said something like, "I can really see us working well together. Don't you think so?" I was to begin the next Monday, February 1. My pay was $12 per hour or about $2,080 a month, gross. My take-home pay was about $388 a week. Pacific Quad had a great medical benefits plan. For a small monthly deduction, the plan paid for almost every medical visit. I only had to pay a $10 deductible, or "co-payment," as they called it, for office visits, and $5 for prescriptions.

Mr. Schmit told me a little about Pacific Quad. The company sold computer software that it had developed and copyrighted. The software was designed to help businesses manage information more efficiently. It seemed to deal mostly with medium-sized companies. Mr. Schmit seemed to be involved only in running the day-to-day affairs of the company, like paying the bills, billing the customers, hiring and firing the office staff, and things like that. I don't think he is a computer "geek," just an office manager. Mr. Walsh was his boss, but they seemed like good friends. They joked around a lot, and I got the feeling that they socialized a lot.

I had a funny feeling about Mr. Schmit, but at that point there really wasn't anything definite that I could put my finger on, so I decided to take the job. After all, I thought, first impressions turn out wrong a lot of the time, and it wasn't really that I felt bad about my interview with him—sort of uneasy would be more like it.

I reported to work the next Monday morning. Mr. Schmit showed me where my desk was, and introduced me to the people in the office. The two other administrative assistants and I worked in a large open area in the middle of the office. I think their names were Joyce Radfield and Liz Morrisey. A four-foot-high partition wall divided up the area into four sections. We each had one section, with a desk and a computer. The fourth section was used for files.

I've seen the diagram of the Pacific Quad office produced by their lawyers (PQ-0001) and it is accurate. The front doors of the office were in the middle of one wall near the other two administrative assistants. There were offices and a lunchroom along the other three walls. The sales staff had offices there too. One salesperson was Gloria Warner. She had an office next to Mr. Schmit. The other two sales reps were in the unmarked offices at the top left of the diagram. I don't remember what their names were. It was two guys. The bookkeeper was Joey something. There was a mail clerk named Sam, I think. Mr. Walsh, one of the owners of the company had his office on the other side of Schmit's. The sales reps were not in the office much. They were usually on the road visiting customers. There were two other owners who did not have offices there. I don't recall their names. I never met them.

Problems with Mr. Schmit

Mr. Schmit's office was the closest to my desk. The door to his office was about ten feet away from my desk. When he was sitting at his desk, he could see me working at my desk if he leaned forward a little. As a matter of fact, a several times during both weeks, when at my desk, I got the feeling that someone was looking at me, and when I turned around, I thought I saw him leaning back away from the door, as if he had been watching me but didn't want me to see that he had been looking.

At the beginning of the first week, I stayed very busy and I didn't really have time to pay much attention to Mr. Schmit. My job was supposed to be to take care of the correspondence and input sales data, and there was a lot to learn and a lot of work piled up for me. I spent most of Monday morning reading some of the incoming e-mail and letters that I was supposed to answer and reading through the "canned" answers that had already been stored on the computer, so that I could get a feeling for what I was supposed to do.

Mr. Schmit came by my desk a few times on Monday and Tuesday and talked to me. I don't really remember exactly what he said. I think it was just, "How's it going?" or, "Got any questions?" The thing that stuck out in my mind, though, even on the first day, was the way he continued to look at me. Just like in the interview, he was leering at me. In a way, it was as if he was sizing me up, from head to toe. Sometimes when I happened to look in his direction, it seemed like he was looking at some part of my body. It was really impersonal—he never looked me in the eye when he had been looking at me that way, but he also didn't look away or seem embarrassed. He just kept looking.

The first week, I kept trying to ignore Mr. Schmit. I really was busy, and I just did not want to start off my new job by having problems with the boss, so I just told myself that it would stop, that everything would be fine after a while.

Just before lunch on Friday of the first week, things got worse. Mr. Schmit asked me if I would like to have lunch with him, and then he said something like, "I really enjoy eating out." He chuckled and had this big grin on his face. Then he gave me a big wink. Then I felt my face get warm, and I didn't really know what to do or say. I told him that I had agreed to meet a friend for lunch, which was not true, but I was so upset I couldn't think of any other way of saying no to him. He said that was too bad because he would like to get to know me better since we would be "working so closely together" as he put it.

I was upset and embarrassed. I wasn't sure if Mr. Schmit was singling me out for attention, or if he acted that way with all the female staff. I decided to not reach any definite conclusions about Mr. Schmit's intentions until I'd worked there longer. However, I had difficulty sleeping that weekend. I kept hearing his suggestive tone of voice and seeing his leering smile. I began to think about quitting, but decided to give it some more time. I thought that if I did not respond to his advances, he'd get the message and stop.

The following Monday, Mr. Schmit was standing in his doorway talking to some of the other employees. I don't really remember who else was there, but they were joking around. Mr. Schmit told a few dirty jokes. I don't really remember exactly what they were, but one of them had to do with women with large breasts. A couple of times, he forwarded some dirty jokes he received via e-mail to all the employees. I guess he thought they were funny and that we'd enjoy them. I was offended and deleted them immediately. I never mentioned to him or anyone else that I did not like those kinds of jokes. I tried to ignore them and do my job. I felt I was too new on the job to complain. The others in the office tended to yuk it up with Schmit, so I didn't think anyone else was offended.

A couple of mornings, after I got to work, he would come up behind me to say something about how nice I looked that day. I guess I must have really been edgy, because he startled me when he said that, and I jumped a little bit. One time, when he saw me jump, he laughed, put his hand on my shoulder and massaged it a little, and said something like, "There, there, I'm not really that scary, am I?" I don't think I said anything then, and he walked away. I did not like him touching me.

The second week just seemed to get worse and worse. He kept looking at me in the same way. It seemed as if he spent most of that week joking around with different people somewhere near my desk, and his sense of humor seemed to focus pretty much on sex and double meanings. I can't remember exactly the words he used, but when they were talking about computers, and he kept talking about them "going down" and "coming up"—and then everyone would nudge each other and laugh. Even when he wasn't talking directly to me like that, I was offended by a lot of what he said. It seemed that it was just normal for him to talk the way I suppose men do in locker rooms—just vulgar most of the time.

Throughout both weeks I worked there, Mr. Schmit would send dirty e-mail jokes to me. I was very offended by them. I kept three of them. I thought that if I saved some of the worst ones, I could show them to Mr. Walsh to illustrate how offensive Mr. Schmit's humor was. I noticed that the jokes were being forwarded to Mr. Walsh too, but I thought I'd better save them in case Mr. Walsh did not see or remember them. I gave copies of my printouts of the e-mails to Ms. Cunningham, the investigator from the Nita Department of Fair Employment.

The second Wednesday, I think, Mr. Schmit came up to my desk and started talking with me. He looked at the papers on my desk, and he said, "Looks like you're getting a little behind in your work. I'd sure like to get a little behind in mine." He asked me if I had a boyfriend. I blushed and said, "No." He gave me a wink as he walked back into his office. Fortunately, it was time for me to go home when he said that, because I was really upset.

All that night, I kept thinking about what was going on, and I doubt that I slept at all. I came to the realization that Mr. Schmit was not going to stop what he was doing to me, and I really didn't know what to do. I wanted to talk to someone at work about it, but there really wasn't anyone that I felt I could talk to. I thought about talking to Mr. Walsh, because he was Mr. Schmit's boss, but I had barely met him, and he didn't seem like someone who would be easy to talk to. Plus, as I've said, he and Mr. Schmit seemed to be close friends. He would probably defend Schmit.

Another thing that Mr. Schmit had been doing was to touch me "accidentally." If we were passing by each other, he always brushed into me, even though there was always enough room for him to get by me without touching me. Once or twice, when he came to my desk to speak to me, he would put his hand on my shoulder or back as he spoke to me. I always got the feeling that he was trying to look down my dress. As politely as I could, I asked Mr. Schmit to, "Please don't do that," to tell him I did not appreciate being touched. Once, he said that it was just an accident. Another time he responded, "Do what?"

Friday morning of the second week, I was there for about an hour before he got there. When he got to the office, he stopped at my desk on the way to his office. He looked at me coldly and said something like, "Well, Alice, when I hired you I was hoping we could work well together. I'm still hoping I was right." When I listened to his tone of voice and looked at him, I understood that he wasn't just talking about my job performance. Shortly after that, he sent me a truly disgusting e-mail "joke" about temporary and permanent secretaries "screwing" on desks. I saved that one to show to Mr. Walsh.

About an hour later, he leaned forward over his desk and called me into his office. I just can't re member his exact words, but he asked me to go out with him that weekend. I said something like, "No, I don't think so," and I asked why. He had a big grin and winked at me and said, "It's business." I asked him what business had to do with us going out on the weekend, and he said, "We'll see what comes up." When he said that, I knew he meant it as a sexual proposition.

I walked out of his office and then sat at my desk, shaking, trying to figure out what to do, when he came out of his office to my desk and started to talk to me. Suddenly, I realized that I just couldn't take any more of it, and I told him that I wasn't going to play his games any more. Without waiting for him to reply, I got up and went out in the hall to take a deep breath. I started crying, so I went into the ladies' room.

After I had calmed down, I decided to go tell Mr. Walsh what was going on. I walked into his office, and explained what had been going on the two weeks I had been there. I showed him the dirty e-mail joke I'd received that morning from Mr. Schmit. It's true that I was upset, but he must have understood what I was saying. He said, "I can't be bothered. If you're not happy working for Mr. Schmit, you can leave and find another job. I know you're wrong, I've known him for years."

At that point, I didn't think I had any choice. Mr. Schmit wasn't going to stop, and Mr. Walsh didn't care. I felt completely helpless and frustrated. I walked to my desk, got my purse, told Mr. Schmit "I'm quitting," and left. About a week later, I received a letter from Mr. Walsh containing a check for two full weeks' work. He said that "under the circumstances," it was "only fair" that I should receive an entire two weeks' pay, $776.00, although I'd left midday the second Friday. I understood him to mean that it was only fair to give me a full two weeks' pay after having been harassed by Mr. Schmit.

The DFEH complaint

About a week after I quit Pacific Quad, I started to get angry. I just couldn't let what Mr. Schmit did to me go. I'd lie awake at night angry and crying. I was seeing Anna Mills two to three times a week for counseling. Finally, near the end of March YR-1, I called the Nita Department of Fair Employment. They told me how to file a formal complaint, and I did. Not long thereafter, I was contacted by a DFEH investigator named Annie Cunningham. She was very nice, very sympathetic. I told her all about what Schmit did to me. She called me several times to update me on the progress of her investigation. At one point, I went into her office and signed a release allowing her to look at my medical records and my employment file at Pacific Quad.

Ultimately, she told me that Pacific Quad refused to settle the case. Walsh refused to pay for my medical and counseling expenses or to give me any money for the mental anguish they caused me. All he offered was a formal apology from Mr. Schmit. That was not good enough. It would let them get away with it. I told Annie Cunningham that that was not adequate.

Around September, YR-1, I received a "right to sue" letter from the DFEH. Since it looked like there was nothing else they could or would do about the matter, I found a lawyer and told him I wanted to sue.

I was never made aware of whether Pacific Quad had a policy against sexual harassment. It was never mentioned to me by anyone. I was never given or asked to read a policy manual or an employee manual. Nor was I ever told of any office procedure for handling such complaints.

I never spoke about Schmit's conduct to the other two administrative assistants at Pacific Quad while I was working there. One, Joyce, had been there for years, so I thought she was probably not offended by Schmit's sexual antics. The other, Liz, like Joyce, seemed to enjoy Schmit's warped sense of humor. Plus, I doubt she saw much of Schmit's harassment of me. In any event, I did not feel that I knew either one of them well enough to speak with them about my problem with Schmit.

The aftermath

All of that was more than a year ago, but it still upsets me to talk or think about it. For a long time, I felt so traumatized. It was all that I thought about for months. I started seeing Anna Mills often—two or three times a week—so that we could talk about my feelings. Between then and now, I've probably paid her more than $8,000 for around 100 visits or more, I don't recall exactly how many. She raised her rates, so I was now paying $75 a session. She kept trying to tell me that not all men were out to take advantage of me, but deep down it took a long time before I could believe that.

I lost all the ground I had gained in counseling after the Melvyl incident. I was a wreck. Those first few months, I had a hard time sleeping, and when I did, I had nightmares about being harassed. I didn't feel I could go out and work. It cost me another, better job.

A week after I left Pacific Quad, I was called by a company with a job offer. I had applied for a job at Quaantum Computers the same time I applied for the Pacific Quad position. Quaantum was still looking and called me. They wanted to hire me as a management trainee. Their director of personnel said that they thought I had great potential. They offered me a salary of $35,000 a year with full medical and retirement benefits. I would have taken the job had I not been so emotionally devastated by Schmit's treatment of me. I was in no condition to go into a new workplace and perform up to my potential. I was a basket case. So, I turned down the job.

Gradually, I began to feel better, and in December of last year I began looking for a job. I called Quaantum, but the management job was filled and they had no other openings. Around mid-January of this year, I began work as an office assistant for Business Systems, Inc., which is an office supply company. I work for the Director of Purchasing, Ms. Susan Lindbloom, at a salary of $10 per hour, or $1,600 per month, gross, which is less than the $2,080 a month I was making at Pacific Quad. Also, BSI has only a major medical insurance plan for its employees. I pay hundreds a month, but it only covers catastrophic illnesses. For everything else, I've got to pay 100 percent out of my own pocket. Still, it was a big relief to be getting a paycheck again, because I had to borrow money from my parents to pay for my counseling and to otherwise get by for the eleven months I wasn't working.

One of these days, I plan to go back and get my degree. This whole business has made that a lot more difficult. Obviously, it caused me a lot of mental anguish. I really wasn't able to do anything for a long time. On top of that, it has caused some serious financial hardships for me. I still owe my parents money from the time when I couldn't work. It will be a long time until I can afford to stop working and go back to school, but I'm still not giving up hope.

Gloria Warner

After I quit Pacific Quad, I heard that Schmit dated Gloria Warner, one of the salespeople at Pacific Quad. I understand from my attorney that Schmit tried to get Gloria into bed but she turned him down. In retaliation, he got her fired. What a jerk he is! With him married and having a teenage son! It proves that I did not imagine Schmit's harassment. He's just another male sexual predator. I'd drop the case if Walsh would fire him. I have not spoken to Gloria Warner since I left Pacific Quad. While I was there, we only exchanged pleasantries. I wasn't her office assistant. I'm sure glad that she had the courage to come forward and tell what she knows about Stanley Schmit.

Statement of Anna Mills

My name is Anna Mills. I live at 1909 Pacific Shores Lane, Nita City, Nita. I am a Licensed Clinical Social Worker. I have master's degrees in social work and counseling. I have worked as a counselor at the Women's Center of Nita State University here in Nita City for the past five years. As a counselor in the Women's Center, I function in several different capacities. First, I provide career counseling for our women students and alumnae. I also run discussion sessions and workshops relating to women's issues. I provide individual personal counseling, and I direct a peer counseling program. Further, I do special counseling for victims of rape and sexual harassment. In this last role, I provide crisis intervention and long-term counseling, and I also advise and assist students who wish to seek official redress for the acts committed against them. I have provided all of these services since assuming my position at the Women's Center.

I first met Alice Rowe in the fall of YR-4. I met her when she came to the Women's Center with a complaint against a professor. I helped her file the complaint and counseled her throughout the investigation. Alice is a very intelligent young woman who is now only a semester away from earning her bachelor of science degree in computer science, but she has repeatedly taken time off from school to work at secretarial jobs. In my opinion, this is not only due to her lack of money, but because of a fear of success and lack of self-esteem. In our counseling sessions, Alice and I discussed both pragmatic career planning goals and strategies and her deep-seated fears and doubts, which were manifested in her academic and personal life.

Although I generally work only with students from the university, I occasionally continue with counseling sessions after students leave the university. The university requires that non-students pay for these sessions. We use a sliding-scale fee schedule. During the second half of YR-2 and January YR-1, Alice's counseling sessions had dropped from once a month to only on an "as needed" basis. In other words, the last half of YR-2, she had made such significant progress that I told her that she should come to see me only when she felt it necessary. I did not see her at all between June of YR-2 and January YR-1. From February YR-1, when the incident at Pacific Quad happened, through October YR-1, Alice came to counseling sessions twice a week, occasionally three times a week. Since the end of October, Alice has been coming to counseling sessions once a week. Since February YR-1, Alice has paid $8,175 (109 sessions at $75 per session) in counseling fees. I raised my fees $10 at the end of YR-2.

During February and the months that followed in YR-1, Alice and I discussed extensively the reported incident of sexual harassment at Pacific Quad. Alice told me that she had been leered at, touched inappropriately, propositioned and otherwise pressured sexually by her supervisor at Pacific Quad, and then forced to resign when she reported the harassment to his supervisor.

The perceived harassment had a serious psychological effect on Alice. She could function on a basic level, but she could not work for many months. She had nightmares and insomnia. The trauma that she felt as a result of the harassment undid much of the progress she and I had made. She is back at work now. I believe she found a job recently. As a college counselor, I have seen many students without a strong sense of confidence. These individuals are less likely to be successful in school and in relationships. Confidence is the most important thing in young people. I was working with Alice on her self-esteem. At one point, she really seemed to embrace her decision to seek a career in the computer industry. Still, she has had difficulty establishing trusting, close relationships with her peers, especially men.

I have Alice's counseling file with me today. There is nothing in the file relating directly to our counseling sessions, as it is not my practice to take notes during or after the sessions. With one exception, the only writing in the file are billing records. The one additional writing in the file is a letter I wrote to a colleague of mine, Saul Jacobs. Saul is a counselor in private practice, and I often ask him to be available for my clients when I go out of town. In the summer of YR-1, I was away at a conference and on vacation for a period of about five weeks, and I asked Saul to fill in for me. When I do this, I sometimes send Saul a description of some of my clients, as a sort of "introduction" to them. I wrote one such memo to Saul concerning Alice. In the letter, I briefly described Alice's situation and my psychological assessment. I used some language in the memo that I now regret, as I now realize that it could be misinterpreted. I never meant to indicate by anything I wrote that I disbelieved Alice's report of sexual harassment at Pacific Quad. I had then, and I have now, full confidence that Alice perceived the situation accurately, and reported it to me truthfully.

Statement of Gloria Warner

Background

My name is Gloria Ann Warner. I live at 355 Linda Mar Road, Nita City, Nita. I am twenty-eight years old. I am single and live alone. I have never been married. I was born and raised in Nita City and graduated from Nita State University with a degree in business administration in YR-5. I took courses in accounting, finance, marketing, organizational behavior, and information management sciences. The latter course got me interested in computers.

I did not work until I graduated from college. My first job after graduation was with CompUSA here in Nita City. I was in "management training" for two years, but I decided that I did not want to run a store that sells home computers. Plus, it looked like it would take too long before I could move into management at the national level. So, near the end of November YR-3, I quit CompUSA and went to work for Pacific Quad here in Nita City. It wasn't exactly what I was looking for, but at Comp USA I found that I was good at sales and had learned a lot about computers.

Current employment

I am currently employed as an outside salesperson for Orange Computers. As an outside sales representative, or "sales rep," my job is to visit potential customers, usually small businesses, after they call the company in response to our advertisements or customer referrals. I look over their present computer system and talk to them about their needs. Often, their computer needs have outgrown their present system and they need an upgrade of computers and/or software, such as to install a "wireless Local Area Network" (a "WiFi LAN") so their employees can communicate with each other from in or out of the office without having to physically plug into the office system or a phone jack. Orange Computers sells its own computer hardware, the Orange Computer, including Orange network "servers" or "routers" (large capacity computers that route e-mail messages, store and back up all of the office computer files, and connect with the Internet and the Web, among other things), and software that we buy from software manufacturers. After I make the sale, the customer signs a contract for one of various levels of products and services. Then we provide a computer engineer to the customer to set up and get running the products the customer purchased from us. We also sell service contracts for ongoing service and troubleshooting. I'm on the road much of the time visiting customers. It usually involves driving to locations in the vicinity of Nita City. Usually I don't travel more than 250 miles from Nita City.

Pacific Quad

I worked as an outside sales representative for Pacific Quad, Inc., from January YR-2 to August 27 YR-1. I was doing essentially the same job that I am now doing for Orange Computers. All of my contact with our customers was at the customer's place of business. Orange Computers and Pacific Quad are competitors to some degree, but Pacific Quad does not sell hardware, only software. Pacific Quad's business was selling its own copyrighted software to solve its customers' information management problems. It usually dealt with medium-sized businesses. I would do a lot of "cold calls" on businesses and try to sell them PQ's software to increase the ease and efficiency with which their computer systems handle their information. After I signed up a business, John Walsh, my supervisor and the creator of some of PQ's software, would consult with the customer and the salesperson about the appropriate software package and recommend necessary additional hardware needs. We didn't sell hardware. PQ only recommended it. Then Walsh or some other PQ "techie" would customize the software to meet the customer's special needs.

While I was there, Pacific Quad employed about twelve people. John Walsh, Wilbur Matthews, and Jason Novak owned the company, but Matthews and Novak did not have offices at Pacific Quad. Apparently, they are the creative "geeks" who invent software on their computers at home. The office personnel, two or three office assistants, a bookkeeper, and a shipping clerk, were supervised by Stan Schmit, who was responsible for the day-to-day operations of the company. John Walsh worked with the customers and supervised the sales staff, of which there were three. All of the employees had offices or cubicles at the PQ office. The diagram of the office (PQ-0001) PQ provided looks correct. The other salespeople used the unmarked offices in the upper left of the diagram. When I was there, the office personnel under Schmit included Joey Lynch, the bookkeeper (he was about forty-five years old, married with kids), a guy named Sam who was the shipping clerk, and two or three office assistants.

The other sales reps at Pacific Quad when I was there included Bob Callahan and George McDermott. When George and I were hired near the end of YR-3, the sales staff was increased to three.

The office assistants at Pacific Quad

There were usually two office assistants employed at PQ. Then, in February YR-1, they added a third. It seems like quite a few assistants worked at Pacific Quad for short periods of time while I was there. Looking at the list of persons employed at Pacific Quad from February 1, YR-2, through March 31, YR-1 (PQ-0005), I recognize the names of several women who were secretaries or office assistants there. My secretary the whole time I was there was Joyce Radville. She was in her early thirties and married. I believe Susan Robinson replaced Alice Rowe. Robinson was in her twenties and single. Chris Kolbus, really just a teenage girl out of high school, was there only a few weeks. Cindy Leonard was older, probably around fiftyish. I think I remember Carolyn Kirk. She was young—in her twenties. Liz Morrisey was there when I left. She is in her thirties.

I recall Carolyn Kirk saying something to the other assistants like, "I don't know how you all can continue working here," on the day she quit. In light of how Stan treated me, Rowe's complaint, and what I saw and heard about Stan, it was clear to me that Kirk couldn't understand how the rest of the women in the office could put up with his testosterone-driven behavior. All of the women in the office were relatively attractive. And no wonder. Schmit hired them. A coincidence? I think not. Let me explain.

Warner's relationship with Stan Schmit

While at Pacific Quad, I was actually in the office only about one-third to one-half of the time. The rest of the time, I was out meeting with clients in their offices. After I was hired at Pacific Quad, I noticed that Schmit was looking at me as if he were undressing me with his eyes. I felt uncomfortable about it, but let it pass without comment. A few months after I began working there, Stan seemed to find a reason to come into my office whenever I was there. He'd ask me about whether my secretary was doing my work adequately and things like that. Soon, he asked me to lunch. Said he liked to get to know the sales staff. I put him off a couple of times, but he was persistent and I finally agreed. I knew he was married with a son, but he's in his late forties and not bad looking. I was single and lonely. I was flattered—at first.

After that, he asked me to lunch almost every day I was in the office. I went with him several times. Eventually, in mid-YR-2, he asked me for a date. When I said I thought he was married, he mumbled something like "in name only." I realized he wanted to begin an affair so declined to go on a date with him. Not that he didn't keep trying for more. But he was married, and—well, not exactly what I was looking for.

Also, I was told by one of the female office assistants, I can't remember who, that Stan was known in the office as a real "Lothario" and that he was none too subtle about it when it came to the women office assistants. He was also pretty crude. In the office, he would often lean over the women while they were sitting at their desks and look down their dresses. He'd compliment them on how the dress or top they were wearing "really showed off" their figure. He'd forward to everyone in the office off-color jokes that he received via e-mail. He seemed to get lots of dirty e-mail jokes.

He also had a tendency to touch you. I mean, the women in the office. He'd come up to you from behind and put his arm around your waist or his hand on your shoulder and say, "Hey, darlin'," and things like that. He called all the women "darlin'." He'd comment on how much he liked your perfume or your hair. I could tell that some of the women were uncomfortable with his touching and frequent off-color jokes. One got the feeling that he was "trolling" for someone who would show some interest in him.

Toward the end of YR-2, I started dating a new guy I really liked and I told Stan that he and I should stop going to lunch and that he should tone it down. I meant that he should stop flirting so much with me. After that, he was pretty cool toward me. He avoided me altogether, which was fine with me until he turned on me. He and John Walsh were good friends—drinking and golfing buddies. I never mentioned anything to Walsh about Stan's conduct toward me or the other women in the office because I knew Walsh would never do anything about it. Plus, if I bad-mouthed Stan to John, John might not like it and he was my boss, if you know what I mean.

Anyhow, during the summer of YR-1, after I rebuffed Stan's advances, I think Stan poisoned my relationship with Walsh by bad-mouthing me behind my back and making it clear to John that he would be happier if I no longer worked there. True, I never heard him do it, and Walsh never told me Stan was talking to him about me. The reason I believe it is that around the same time, Walsh began requiring me to be on the road more and work longer hours, and Walsh started complaining about my work for the first time.

Finally, in August YR-1, I was asked by a friend who worked for Orange Computers if I wanted to apply for a sales rep job that just opened there. Because of the tension between me and Stan at the office, because I thought Stan was trying to undermine me with Walsh, and because of the increased work and pressure, I applied for the job at Orange Computers. I was quickly hired, starting September 1, YR-1.

I was not fired by Pacific Quad. I was not told that I should look for another job or be fired. They had no reason to fire me. I always did my job and never missed an appointment with a customer. True, my sales were down. But the industry had gotten more competitive that year, so everyone's sales were down. I didn't like the extra pressure Walsh was putting on me. The Orange Computer job looked less stressful, and I didn't suffer a pay cut, which was, like at Pacific Quad, a mix of a salary plus commissions and a possible bonus for exceeding certain expectations. I was making about $60,000 to 65,000 a year at PQ.

Pacific Quad did not have a system of formal employee evaluations, so I can't show you that I was considered a good, productive sales rep until the mid-to-end of the summer of YR-1. Nevertheless, until the summer of YR-1, Walsh had only good things to say about my work. I believe that Walsh highly recommended me when the people at Orange Computers called him for a reference.

I was not aware of any formal policy against sexual harassment or discrimination at Pacific Quad. The place was pretty informal. They didn't have an employee handbook or manual of any kind. I never heard either Schmit or Walsh or anyone else in the office talk about a company anti-harassment policy.

Alice Rowe

My office at Pacific Quad was right next to Mr. Schmit's office. The walls of the offices are pretty thin, so sometimes I could hear conversations in his office when the rest of the office was not too noisy.

One day in early February YR-1, I was sitting in my office when I heard Schmit say to John Walsh, "Hey, I've just hired a real babe as my secretary." Walsh said in response, "Good luck, you devil, you." They both laughed. I did not hear either one of them specifically mention Alice Rowe's name, but Alice was the only person hired around the time I heard the remark, so I am sure that they were talking about her.

I never saw Schmit "hit on" Alice Rowe, or anything like that. She seemed to be a very quiet, private person. I wasn't sure if that was the way she always was or whether it was because she was new to the office. Anyhow, I never saw Schmit act inappropriately with Alice, nor did she ever mention to me that she was having problems with him. As I said, I wasn't in the office that much the two weeks or so she was there. I don't think I was in the office the day she quit.

I first heard that Alice filed a complaint about sexual harassment at the beginning of the summer, a few months after she left Pacific Quad. Stan Schmit stopped Walsh outside my office and said loudly, "Remember that hysterical chick Rowe, you know, the one that was only here for about a week? Well, would you look at this garbage—now she thinks that I wanted to go to bed with her. That crazy broad!" That's the way Stan talks. He refers to women as "chicks" and "broads." Another reason I would never date him.

Warner's call to DFEH

I have been asked to testify for Alice by her lawyer. I told him I would. He contacted me after learning that I had called the Nita State Department of Fair Employment and Housing after I learned that Alice Rowe had filed a sexual harassment complaint with them. After I heard Schmit tell Walsh about Rowe's complaint, I looked up the number for the Fair Employment Department and called them. I spoke to the investigator who was handling Alice's file—a Ms. Cunningham. I reported what I heard Schmit say to Walsh about "hiring a babe." I didn't tell Cunningham that I went on lunch dates with Schmit. I saw no reason to go into that. I called because I feel that men like Stan Schmit should not be allowed to get away with their predatory practices. He and Walsh were buddies, so he wasn't going to put a stop to it. I'm glad that Alice Rowe has filed her lawsuit.

I would never file a complaint with the DFEH myself. I didn't leave PQ because of sexual harassment. Stan just retaliated against me. Anyway, if I were to file a harassment complaint or lawsuit, I'd be a marked woman for the rest of my career. Good luck finding another job if it is known that I was the kind of female who cried sexual harassment or sexual discrimination against some crude co-employee. I don't doubt that Alice has a good case, however. I hope she socks it to them.

Documents
Available to All Sides

Office Floor Plan of Pacific Quad, Inc.

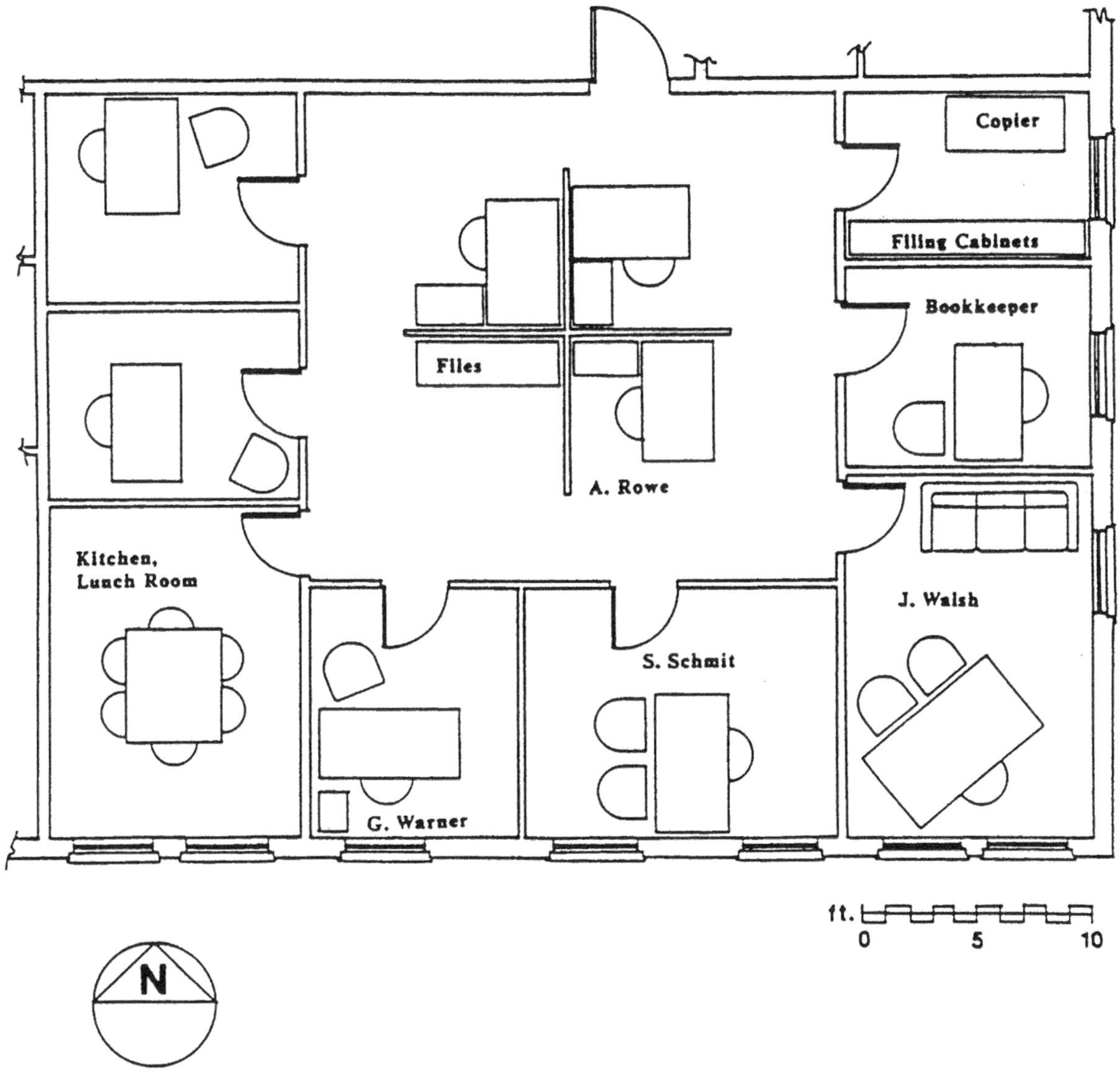

PQ-0001

BENJAMIN J. COHEN

Attorney at Law
1341 Haven Court Nita City, Nita 99990
(721) 555-0479

January 25, YR-0

Henry Glenn, Esq. Glenn & O'Malley
100 Zee Street, Suite 801
Nita City, Nita 99990

RE: Alice Rowe v. Pacific Quad, Inc.

Dear Mr. Glenn:

In response to your Request to Produce Documents dated January 20, YR-0, I am enclosing two documents. One is a document entitled "COMPLAINT FORM" and the other is a document entitled "DECISION." Although I am certainly not willing to stipulate to the admissibility of the two documents, I am willing to stipulate that they are true and accurate copies of authentic business records of Nita State University.

Sincerely,

Benjamin J. Cohen

Benjamin J. Cohen

BJC:ak

Encls.

AR-0001

NITA STATE UNIVERSITY
Student Grievance Board
Complaint Form

Please answer all of the following questions. Please type or print legibly in ink.

1. Name:

Alice Rowe

2. Local Address & Telephone:

1040 Redwood Lane Nita City, Nita 99990 (721) 555-1047

3. Permanent Address & Telephone:

Same as #2

4. Against whom is this grievance being filed *(please give full name & department)*:

James Melvyl, Associate Professor, Dept. of History

5. Please describe in detail the circumstances and events which led to your filing this complaint. Try to be precise about the dates of discrete events. Use the back of this form for additional information.

I am currently enrolled in Prof. Melvyl's class "American History Through Literature." It is a small seminar; there are only about thirteen students. I began to notice at the beginning of the semester that Prof. Melvyl likes to stare at me intensely. He also makes sexual jokes (over)

6. Please identify any persons who witnessed the events described above, who you believe would corroborate the allegations you have made here. Continue on the back of the form if necessary.

I am certain that all of the students in Prof. Melvyl's class will verify what I have said concerning Prof. Melvyl's conduct in the classroom. There are no witnesses, however, (over)

SIGNATURE Alice Rowe DATE 10-27-YR-4

AR-0002

Grievance Board Complaint Form Attachment

#5 (cont)

in class, mostly puns, and he always looks in my direction when doing so. I am certain that I am not mistaken about his behavior. It is so obvious that all of the students know what is going on.

I have been trying to ignore Prof. Melvyl's treatment of me, which I found offensive, humiliating, and degrading, but it has become impossible to do so any longer. Three weeks ago I was in his office discussing my paper for the course and he asked me to go out with him. Of course I said no. Later, when I confronted him, he denied the entire incident.

#6 (cont)

to Prof. Melvyl's attempt to proposition me in his office. I did relate this experience to Anna Mills, a counsulor at the Women's Center, soon after it happened. I'm certain that she will corroborate how upset it made me.

AR-0003

NITA STATE UNIVERSITY

Student Grievance Board Decision

Complaining student:	Alice Rowe
Complaint against:	James Melvyl, Associate Professor, Department of History
Nature of complaint:	Sexual Harassment
Date of complaint:	October 27, YR-4

Having investigated the complaint made by Ms. Rowe against Professor Melvyl, including interviews of both parties and other witnesses, it is the decision of the board that Ms. Rowe's complaint is not supported by sufficient evidence to justify further proceedings.

However, in view of the obvious strains that this complaint has put on the teacher/student relationship between Professor Melvyl and Ms. Rowe, it is the recommendation of this board that Ms. Rowe should be permitted, if she chooses, to withdraw from Professor Melvyl's course, and that Ms. Rowe's petition to withdraw from the course should be treated as if it had been filed before the November 1 deadline if she files it within 10 days of this decision.

The complaint is DISMISSED.

November 15, YR-4

AR-0004

Alice Rowe

1040 Redwood Lane Nita City, Nita
(721) 555-1047

Work Experience

* Leviathan Computers, 2600 Industrial Way, Nita City, Nita.
  Program Assistant
  January–August YR-2.

* Starbuck Software, 5301 Wharf Boulevard, Nita City, Nita.
  Administrative Assistant
  January–August YR-3.

* Nita Marine Insurance Company, 100 Ring Road, Nita City, Nita.
  Administrative Assistant
  September YR-5–July YR-4.

* GAM Software, 53 53rd Street, Nita City, Nita.
  Administrative Assistant
  January–August YR-5.

Skills

* Proficient in Microsoft Office applications, Apple applications, Adobe Acrobat PDF, Photoshop, graphic web design, LINXUS,OS/2.

Education

* Nita State University, Nita City, Nita. Completed 105 of 120 units required for BS in Computer Science. Grade point average 3.5.

* Central High School, Nita City, Nita. Diploma awarded, YR-10. National Honor Society.

PQ-0002

PACIFIC QUAD, INC.
A NEW WAVE IN COMPUTERS 24 Beach Avenue Nita City, Nita 99998 (721) 555-5530

APPLICATION FOR EMPLOYMENT

1. Name: Alice Rowe
2. Address and Telephone: 1040 Redwood Lane, Nita City, Nita 99990 (721)555-1047
3. Sex: ( ) M (✓) F 4. Age: YR-26
5. Marital Status: Single (✓) Married ( ) Divorced ( ) Separated ( )
6. Position sought: Secretary
7. Salary desired: Negotiable
8. Relevant educational and career experience: I have completed 105 out of 120 credits necessary for a B.S. in Computer Science at Nita State University. I graduated from Central High School, Nita City, in YR-10. (over)
9. How did you learn of the job opening? A friend of mine saw your advertisement
10. Have you ever been convicted for a criminal offense other than a traffic violation?
    Yes ( ) No (✓) If yes, please explain: ______
11. Are you under the care of a physician? Yes ( ) No (✓) A psychotherapist? Yes ( ) No ( )
    If so, please explain: ______

Please use the remaining space (and the reverse of this form, if necessary) to tell us anything else that you feel is relevant to your application for employment with Pacific Quad, Inc., or to further explain any answers given above.

I would like a career in the computer field and I feel that experience at Pacific Quad would be a good step towards that goal.

PQ-0003

I hereby certify that all statements on this application are true and complete to the best of my knowledge and belief. If employed, I understand that any falsification of the above record may be considered cause of termination.

Date 1-29-YR-1 Signature Alice Rowe

#8 (cont.)

I have been employed as a secretary by various local firms (mostly computer firms) over the last five years. Please refer to my resumé for further details.

PQ-0004

PACIFIC QUAD, INC.

A NEW WAVE IN COMPUTERS 24 Beach Avenue Nita City, Nita 99998 (721) 555-5530

List of Permanent Employees
During the Period of
February 1, YR-2 through March 31, YR-1*

John Walsh (President)
2767 Gold Coast Cir., Nita City, Nita
(8/YR-3 – present)

Wilbur Matthews (Director)
10006 Rolling Hills Ln, North Nita, Nita
(8/YR-3 – present)

Jason Novak (Director)
901 Beach Drive, Nita Beach, Nita
(8/YR-3 – present)

Stanley Schmit (Operations Mgr.)
3215 Bonnet Shores Dr., Nita City, Nita
(8/YR-3 – present)

Robert Callahan (Sales Rep.)
557A Keeton Dr., Nita City, Nita
(9/14/YR-3 – present)

Richard Favorite (Sales Rep.)
8753 Rocky Road, Upper Nita, Nita
(9/13/YR-1 – present)

Sam Frigate (Shipping Clerk)
10115 I-27 Frontage Rd., Apt. 21, Nita City, Nita
(7/4/YR-2 – present)

Carolyn Kirk (Administrative Assistant)
2235 Pierre Dr., Nita City, Nita
(3/24/YR-2 – 5/2/YR-2)

Chris Kolbus (Administrative Assistant)
8909 E. Webster Pike, Nita City, Nita
(6/10/YR-10 – 6/25/YR-2)

Cindy Leonard (Administrative Assistant)
619 Benito Cerino Rd., Nita City, Nita
(1/10/YR-2 – 3/17/YR-2)

Joey Lynch (Bookkeeper)
8631 Market Rd., Lower Nita, Nita
(8/17/YR-3 – present)

George McDermott (Sales Rep.)
267 Disco Lane, Nita City, Nita
(1/20/YR-2 – present)

Liz Morrisey (Administrative Assistant)
971 Peaceful Valley Way, Outer Nita, Nita
(5/17/YR-2 – present)

Joyce Radville (Administrative Assistant)
1427 Baker St., Nita City, Nita
(8/15/YR-3 – present)

Susan Robinson (Administrative Assistant)
375 Bonnet Court, Nita City, Nita
(2/16/YR-1 – present)

Alice Rowe (Administrative Assistant)
1040 Redwood Lane, Nita City, Nita
(2/1/YR-1 – 2/12/YR-1)

Gloria Warner (Sales Rep.)
925 Ocean Way Nita City, Nita
(1/4/YR-2 – 8/27/YR-1)

* This list includes both present and former employees with their last known home address as of October 1, YR-1, and their dates of employment at Pacific Quad. This document was produced by Pacific Quad, Inc., on January 25, YR-0, in response to a written interrogatory submitted by the plaintiff's attorney.

PQ-0005

PACIFIC QUAD, INC.

A NEW WAVE IN COMPUTERS 24 Beach Avenue Nita City, Nita 99998 (721) 555-5530

February 16, YR-1

Alice Rowe
1040 Redwood Lane
Nita City, Nita

Dear Ms. Rowe:

I am sorry that you will not be able to continue as a secretary with us. Even though you did not work a full day on Friday, February 12th, we have decided to pay you for the full two weeks' work. We think that this is only fair, under all of the circumstances. Accordingly, please find enclosed a check for $776.00. Best wishes in your future employment.

Sincerely,

John Walsh

President

JW:jr

Encl: salary check for $776.00

PQ-0006

DEPARTMENT OF FAIR EMPLOYMENT AND HOUSING

PRE-COMPLAINT QUESTIONNAIRE/EMPLOYMENT

The information requested on this form will help us to help you. There is no guarantee that the information submitted will constitute a basis for filing a formal complaint. If you need assistance in preparing this form, please ask the receptionist. When completed, give the form to the receptionist.

FOR OFFICIAL USE ONLY

Name of Interviewer: Annie Cunningham

Date of Interview: March 23, YR-1

PLEASE PRINT

Name: Alice (First) ______ (Middle) Rowe (Last)

Address: 1040 Redwood Lane (Street) ______ (Apt. #)

City: Nita City County: Nita Zip: 99990

Telephone Number: Work ( ) ______ Ext. ______

Home (721) 555-1047

I prefer to be contacted by phone at work ______ at home X days ______

Name: Samuel C. Rowe Telephone: (721) 555-1047
(Person to contact if you cannot be reached)

I wish to complain against: (Name of employer, city, county, agency, etc.)

Name of Employer: Pacific Quad, Inc.

Street Address: 24 Beach Avenue

City: Nita City County: Nita Zip: 99990

Telephone Number: (721) 555-5530 Number of Employees: 12

Others: ______

Street Address: ______

City: ______ County: ______ Zip: ______

DFEH-0001

1. I was discriminated against because of my (check only those which apply):

____ Race	____ Color	____ National Origin/Ancestry
X___ Sex	____ Age (over 40)	____ Marital Status
____ Medical Condition	____ Physical Handicap	____ Religion

2. How do you feel you were discriminated against

X___ Termination	____ Denied Employment	X___ Harassment
X___ Differential Treatment	____ Denied Promotion	____ Other (Please Specify)

3. What reasons were given by the employer for the action taken against you?
None given.

4. Date of alleged discrimination: February 1-12, YR-1

5. What remedy are you seeking through DFEH?
Stop the harassment, damages for my trauma, backpay until I can go back to work, and pay my medical bills.

6. Employment date:
A. Date Hired: 1/29/YR-1
Job Title: Administrative Assistant
B. Date of Termination: 2/12/YR-1
Job title at time of discrimination: Administrative Assistant
C. Salary of position in question: $2,080/mo.
D. Name of immediate supervisor: Stanley Schmit
E. Is there a union? No If so, name the union and local # ________

F. Have you filed a union grievance? No If so, name the union and local # ________

G. Have you attempted to resolve your problem by discussing the matter with a representative of management? Yes
If so, name the parties contacted: I talked to both Mr. Schmit and John Walsh.

H. If terminated, have you since been employed? Yes ______ No X
Name of company: ________ Date of hire: ________
Job Title: ________ Salary: ________

DFEH-0002

7. What information do you have to indicate that you were treated differently because of discrimination?

I was hired as an administrative assistant but when I reported to work, I was continually harassed by Mr. Schmit, my supervisor. By the end of the second week, I couldn't put up with him anymore. Then he propositioned me and so I told him that I didn't have to tolerate such treatment. When I complained, they only told me to leave so I did.

8. List the names, job titles and telephone numbers (if possible) of witnesses you feel could provide evidence in your support.

Name	Title	Telephone Numbers Home	Work
Anna Mills	Counselor		(721)555-0038

9. Did you file a complaint with EEOC before coming to this agency? Yes _ No X

10. Complaints other than marital status, medical condition and physical handicap filed with DFEH are often simultaneously filed with the Equal Employment Opportunity Commission of the federal government. (Employer must have sixteen or more employees) and alleged act must have occurred within three hundred days of filing.) In no way does this delay the complaint being processed by this agency. If your complaint is accessed by DFEH, do you wish a copy forwarded to EEOC?
Yes X No ______

11. Have you filed with any other group or agency? Yes ______ No X
If so, name, address, and telephone numbers are requested.

12. Do you have an attorney? Yes ______ No X
If so, please provide name, address, and telephone number.

DFEH-0003

PERSONAL DATA

13. For research purposes, please provide us with the following information:

ETHNIC GROUP:

Black ______ Hispanic _____ Asian _______ Filipino ______Anglo X______

Native American ______ Other Minority (Please Specify) ____________

SEX: Female __X____ Male ________

AGE: __26_____

14. I learned about the Department of Fair Employment and Housing from:

Newspaper __________ Radio ______ TV _________ Bus/BART Ad ______ Poster X_____

Friend Prior Contact with DFEH _________________ Other Government Agency __________

Community Organizations (Please Specify) ________________________________

Other (Please Specify) ______________________________________

(Do Not Write in This Area)

INTERVIEWER'S NOTES

Ms. Rowe alleges sexual harassment during her two weeks of work at Pacific Quad, Inc. Ms. Rowe alleges that her immediate supervisor, Stanley Schmit, propositioned her on Friday, February 12. When Ms. Rowe complained about the harassment and demanded that Mr. Schmit stop such behavior, Mr. Schmit refused and Ms. Rowe left the office. She believes that she was forced to leave. Ms. Rowe does not remember the words of the proposition but remembers that Mr. Schmit had a big smile on his face and a leering look in his eyes.

DFEH-0004

DEPARTMENT OF FAIR EMPLOYMENT AND HOUSING

CASE DIARY
Alice Rowe
#FEP 03-02-A0-000se

Complainant Alice Rowe

Case ____________________

Message Telephone (   ) ____________________

EEOC/HUD# ____________________

Filing Date March 23, YR-1

Service Date ____________________

Respondent Pacific Quad, Inc.

Co-Respondent ____________________

Respondent Contact Person:

Name John Walsh

Title President

Address 24 Beach Avenue, Nita City

Telephone (721) 555-5530

Co-respondent Contact Person:

Name ____________________

Title ____________________

Address ____________________

Telephone ( ) ____________________

Respondent's formal representative to receive closure letter:

Name ____________________

Title ____________________

Address ____________________

Complainant's Change of address #1:

Date notified ____________________

Address ____________________

Telephone (   ) ____________________

Complainant's Change of address #2:

Date notified ____________________

Address ____________________

Telephone (   ) ____________________

ACTIVITY CODES:

IN INVESTIGATION—Begins when complaint is filed and includes activities with sole purpose of obtaining information on case for closure or accusation, including interrogatories and subpoenas.

S/C SETTLEMENT/CONCILIATION—Includes activities involved in reaching a settlement prior to submittal for accusation.

RW REPORT WRITING—Includes progress memos and closing reports.

PH PUBLIC HEARING—Activities performed after a case has been referred to legal for accusation

TIME—To be entered in increments of no less than 15 minutes.

DFEH-0005

Date & Initials	Case activity	Activity Code	Time Hr/Min
YR-1			
3/23	complaint filed served		
4/6	rec'd response to service letter from Walsh		
4/20	called Walsh RE: anti-harassment policy; explained DFEH procedures		
4/22	called complainant to update on case		
4/26	called Walsh RE: respondent's account of facts		
5/3	complainant came into office to sign Release forms, denies Walsh's account of facts		
5/5	called Anna Mills complainant's counselor; will help in any way she can		
5/17	called Walsh RE: settlement possibilities (talked to Robinson—doesn't remember Walsh ever asking her to correct any mistakes in first letter to DFEH)		
6/21	rec'd Walsh letter and Robinson affidavit		
8/30	rec'd call from Gloria Warner		
9/10	issued right-to-sue letter to complainant		
9/17	rec'd call from B. Cohen. Claims he will soon be filing private action for complainant. I told him that when he did I will close case.		
11/23	closed case—complainant elected court action.		

Total Time

District Office Time (record in total hours and/or minutes) Legal Time Total

IN= ________ S/C= _______ RW= _______ PH= _______ ____________ ____________

DFEH-0006

CHARGE OF DISCRIMINATION

This form is affected by the Privacy Act of 1974; see Privacy Act Statement on reverse before completing this form.

ENTER CHARGE NUMBER FEP 03-02 AO 000se EEOC N/A

Nita Department of Fair Employment and Housing and EEOC
(State or local Agency, if any)

Name (Indicate Mr., Ms., or Mrs.) Home telephone No.

Ms. Alice Rowe (721) 555-1047

Address	City	State	County
1040 Redwood Lane	Nita City	Nita	Nita

NAMED IS THE EMPLOYER, LABOR ORGANIZATION, EMPLOYMENT AGENCY, APPRENTICESHIP COMMITTEE, STATE OR LOCAL GOVERNMENT AGENCY WHO DISCRIMINATED AGAINST ME (If more than one list below.)

Name	No. of Employees/Members	Telephone (area Code)
Pacific Quad, Inc.	12	(721) 555-5530

Address	City	State	County
24 Beach Avenue	Nita City	Nita	Nita

Name	No. of Employees/Members	Telephone (area Code)

Address	City	State	County

Cause of discrimination based on: *(Check appropriate boxes)*

☐ Race ☐ Color ☒ Sex ☐ Religion ☐ National Origin ☐ Age

☐ Retaliation ☐ Other *(Specify)* __________

Date most recent or continuing discrimination took place (mo., day, year)

Feb. 12, YR-1

DFEH-0007

The particulars are (if additional space is needed, attach extra sheets)

1. On Friday, January 29, YR-1, I applied for and was hired for the position of administrative assistant at Pacific Quad, Inc. I was interviewed by the operations manager, Stanley Schmit.

2. When I reported to work the next Monday, February 1, YR-1, Mr. Schmit, my immediate supervisor, began sexually harassing me. This harassment continued the entire time I was there. The harassment included the following:

   A. Mr. Schmit propositioned me and used sexual innuendoes.

   B. Mr. Schmit was watching me very closely. I felt that his eyes were constantly on my body.

3. As a woman, I refuse to be subjected to such abuse and demanded that Mr. Schmit stop his harassment. When he refused to do so, I spoke with Mr. Schmit's supervisor, the president of the company, Mr. John Walsh. Mr. Walsh refused to discipline Mr. Schmit and told me to leave.

☒ I also want this charge filed with the EEOC. I will advise the agencies if I change my address or telephone number and I will cooperate fully with them in the processing of my charge in accordance with their procedures.

I declare under penalty of perjury that the foregoing is true and correct.

I swear or affirm that I have read the above charge and that it is true to the best of my knowledge, information and belief.

SIGNATURE OF COMPLAINANT

Alice Rowe

NOTARY (when necessary to meet state and local requirements)

SUBSCRIBED AND SWORN TO BEFORE ME THIS DATE

____

My Commission Expires:

____

DFEH-0008

PACIFIC QUAD, INC.

A NEW WAVE IN COMPUTERS 24 Beach Avenue Nita City, Nita 99998 (721) 555-5530

April 2, YR-1

Ms. Annie Cunningham
Department of Fair Employment & Housing
30 Van Ness Avenue
Nita City, Nita 99990

Dear Ms. Cunningham:

I have received the discrimination complaint from your office, but I frankly do not understand what the problem is. Our records do show that Alice Rowe worked for us for two weeks in February, but she quit without any explanation, not because of any sexual harassment. I have spoken to my operations manager, Stanley Schmit, about Ms. Rowe and he has assured me that discrimination had nothing to do with Ms. Rowe's abrupt departure. Stan never propositioned Ms. Rowe or sexually harassed her.

I personally never knew that Ms. Rowe had any complaints until I talked to Stan on Friday afternoon, February 12th. I rarely talked with her, and didn't see her at all on that day. Stan told me that she'd left but he didn't know why and that he had just assumed that she had decided not to work here after all—secretaries are often like that. You can see that we are very surprised by this complaint.

Frankly, I am very disturbed by this discrimination charge because we have a very strong anti-harassment policy here at Pacific Quad. This company was started by me and two other friends from BMI in August YR-3. I am the principal shareholder and am responsible for the general operations of the company. Thus, you can see that I take this matter personally. I am very disturbed that someone with an overactive imagination would accuse us of such behavior. We are still a very small company of twelve employees, and we like to think of ourselves as a family. This charge has disrupted our work environment and has already taken up a lot of precious time and energy. I would like to cooperate with you in any way I can to resolve this unfortunate misunderstanding. Please feel free to contact me directly if you have any further questions.

Sincerely,

John Walsh

John Walsh

President

JW:sr

DFEH-0009

Investigator's Notes

Annie Cunningham

DATE: April 20, YR-1

CASE: Rowe/Pacific Quad, Inc.

FEP 03-02 A0-OOOse

called John Walsh RE: his response letter of April 2

explained case still open/active and am proceeding with investigation

asked whether his "anti-harassment policy" was in writing; he replied that it was not but that it had often been discussed informally; that the company was "very sensitive to the needs of modern women"

asked whether Pacific Quad had any documentary evidence to support their denial of discrimination; Walsh responded that he didn't remember the details himself and that since Pacific Quad was a small and new company, didn't really have any past resignations or terminations; expressed concern about the privacy of employee records

tried to explain the importance of the submission of some documentary evidence, especially regarding the reason why complainant resigned—Walsh was confused about DFEH authority to investigate/prosecute explained investigatory/conciliation powers and accusation/hearing process

Walsh expressed a desire to avoid any litigation/publicity; didn't think the matter was that serious but wanted to cooperate; said that he would try to gather some documentary evidence and will send to DFEH as soon as possible

DFEH-0010

Investigator's Notes

Annie Cunningham

DATE: April 22, YR-1

CASE: Rowe/Pacific Quad, Inc.

FEP 03-02 A0-OOOse

called complainant Alice Rowe to give her an update on the case

informed her of Walsh's response of April 2 and telephone conversation with Walsh on April 20th

Rowe strongly denies that she quit without giving Schmit or Walsh any reason; says she plainly told Schmit after he propositioned her on Friday, "I don't have to put up with this—I'm not going to play your games."

Rowe also strongly denies that Walsh didn't know about her complaint of sexual harassment; says she went to Walsh's office after Schmit propositioned her on Friday, February 12th; she showed him some of Schmit's "dirty e-mails;" however, Walsh told her, "if you're not happy, you can leave."—Rowe left

Rowe claims to have saved some of Schmit's e-mail and will send them to me. Says she forgot she had them

Rowe denies that there was any anti-harassment policy—she never saw any in writing and never heard of one

Rowe has been seeing a counselor to help her overcome the trauma—she has been told to stay off work for now

DFEH-0011

Investigator's Notes

Annie Cunningham

DATE: April 26, YR-1

CASE: Rowe/Pacific Quad, Inc.

FEP 03-02 A0-OOOse

called Walsh RE: phone conversation with complainant on April 22nd

Walsh admits that he talked to Rowe on Friday, February 12th and says that he had told his secretary Susan to change the sentence in the letter about not knowing anything about Rowe's resignation; says things have been very busy around the office and he hasn't been concentrating on the complaint

Walsh now remembers that Rowe came into his office at around noon on Friday, February 12th, the last day that Rowe worked; Walsh says that Rowe was very upset—her eyes were very wet and red and it looked as if she had been crying

Walsh couldn't quite understand everything Rowe said—began mumbling and sobbing at the same time—maybe something about her not being able to get along with men and that "this always happens to me;" Walsh says that he was pretty confused and didn't know what she was talking about but that eventually she calmed down

Walsh asked if there was anything he could do and suggested that she could leave for a break—he thought that maybe the fresh air would help her and it was time for her lunch break anyway; Walsh strongly denies suggesting that she quit

Walsh says that Rowe never came back—when he didn't see her at her desk later that afternoon, Walsh asked Schmit about her and Schmit said that she had told him that she was quitting, without giving any reason; Schmit thought that maybe she had some personal problems and just couldn't handle the job because she had been agitated since she started

Walsh again denies that there was any harassment

DFEH-0012

Investigator's Notes

Annie Cunningham

DATE: May 3, YR-1

CASE: Rowe/Pacific Quad, Inc.

FEP 03-02 A0-OOOse

Complainant came in to sign release forms (for work-related and medical records); she brought copies of e-mails she received from Schmit

discussed with Complainant the phone conversation with Walsh on April 26; Complainant denies that she was hysterical or incomprehensible—states that if she was upset, it was because of the entire week of harassment and the proposition by Schmit

Asked Complainant for more details about the harassment; Schmit constantly commented on how she looked—how he liked a certain dress or outfit; it was his tone of voice and the look in his eyes that made her feel that he was making sexual innuendoes

Once, Schmit said something about her work, but there were sexual innuendoes about her doing a "good job"

Schmit would often use sexually explicit language in instructions or just in casual conversations with the Complainant, in reference to items that the company developed or just in his expressions; Rowe found his language vulgar and offensive

Complainant also detailed the proposition on Friday; Schmit said something about asking her to go out to dinner or for drinks—she can't remember the exact words but does remember that Schmit was leering and winking; when she refused and asked why, Schmit said, "It's business."

Complainant asked what kind of business required that they go out for dinner over the weekend; Schmit said, "We'll see what comes up"—Complainant interpreted this as a sexual proposition

Complainant admits that she had been crying before going in to see Walsh; she did not go directly from her desk to Walsh's office but stopped at the bathroom first

Complainant vehemently denies that Walsh did not understand her; states that she made it quite clear that she was leaving because of Schmit's harassment

Complainant states that she felt forced to leave the job; that after talking to Walsh, she was so disgusted and frustrated that she simply picked up her purse and told Schmit, "I'm quitting" and then left

Asked Complainant for more details about Schmit's language, expressions, propositions; she said this was all she could recall—became upset at me and accused me of not believing her

DFEH-0013

Investigator's Notes

Annie Cunningham

DATE: May 17, YR-1

CASE: Rowe v. Pacific Quad, Inc.

FEP 03-02 A0-OOOse

called Walsh RE: settlement possibilities explained to Walsh that the key to settlement was:

1) formal institution of an anti-harassment policy

2) back pay, out-of-pocket medical expenses and some compensatory damages for Complainant

Walsh rejected any monetary damages; said he would have Schmit write a formal apology to Rowe and that he would sign it—but that's all

Walsh stated that "maybe Stan uses some colorful language—so what?" and that Schmit never intended to offend or embarrass anyone

Walsh also continues to deny that any propositioning or harassment took place—attributes Rowe's account to her overactive imagination; that "just being friendly" is not harassment

told Walsh that DFEH would continue to gather evidence and investigate but would also continue to be open to settlement offers

DFEH-0014

Investigator's Notes

Annie Cunningham

DATE: August 30, YR-1

CASE: Rowe/Pacific Quad, Inc.

FEP 03-02 A0-OOOse

rec'd call from Gloria Warner RE: Rowe case

Warner is a sales representative at Pacific Quad

found out about complaint because Stanley Schmit came over to her desk and showed her a copy of it

Warner remembers a conversation between Schmit and John Walsh at around the same time Rowe was hired—Schmit told Walsh, "Hey, I've just hired a real hot babe as my secretary"—Warner is pretty sure that Schmit was referring to Rowe but cannot be positive—can't remember the exact dates involved

Warner looked up DFEH phone number in phone book because she thought the information might help—doesn't remember anything else about Rowe

Warner did not want to answer questions about whether she herself had experienced any sexual advances at Pacific Quad but she said that she often felt that Stanley Schmit was "undressing" all of the women with his eyes; does not know of any other cases or complaints of harassment at Pacific Quad

DFEH-0015

From: sschmit@PacQuad.com

To: jwalsh, sfrigate, jlynch, jradville, arowe, lmorrisey

Sent: 2/3/YR-1

Subject: Enjoy
——————————————————-Forward Header——————————————————

From: G_C_HONICK@BURTONCONSTR.HR.COM

To: sschmit@PacQuad.com, jcollins@aol.com,slink@clestica.com

Sent: 2/3/YR-1

Subject: Note from Human Resources
————————————————-Forwarded Message——————————————————

> *A new chemical element has recently been discovered. Here for the first time is a description of its*
> *properties:*

> *Element Name: WOMAN*

> *Symbol: WO*

> *Atomic Weight: (don't even go there!)*

> *Physical Properties: Generally round in form. Boils at nothing and may freeze any time. Melts*
> *whenever treated properly. Very bitter if not used well.*

> *Chemical Properties: Very active. Highly unstable. Possess strong affinity to gold, silver,*
> *platinum, and precious stones. Violent when left alone. Able to absorb great amounts of exotic*
> *food. Turns slightly green when placed next to a better specimen.*

> *Usage: Highly ornamental. An extremely good catalyst for dispersion of wealth. Probably the*
> *most powerful income reducing agent known.*
> *Caution: Highly explosive in inexperienced hands.*

>

DFEH-0016

>

> *A drunk gets up from the bar and heads for the bathroom. A few minutes later, a loud, blood*
> *curdling scream is heard coming from the bathroom. A few minutes after that another loud*
> *scream reverberates through the bar.*

> *The bartender goes into the bathroom to investigate what the drunk is screaming about. "What's*
> *all the screaming about in there? You're scaring my customers!" "I'm just sitting here on the*
> *toilet and every time I try to flush, something comes up and squeezes the hell out my balls."*

> *With that the bartender opens the door, looks in and says, "You idiot! You're sitting on the mop*
> *bucket!!!"*

>

------------------------------------End forwarded Message------------------------------------

DFEH-0017

From: sschmit@PacQuad.com

To: jwalsh, sfrigate, jlynch, jradville, arowe, lmorrisey

Sent: 2/3/YR-1

Subject: Enjoy

——————————————————-Forward Header——————————————————

From: G_C_HONICK@BURTONCONSTR.HR.COM

To: sschmit@PacQuad.com, jcollins@aol.com,slink@clestica.com

Sent: 2/3/YR-1

Subject: Note from Human Resources

————————————————-Forwarded Message——————————————————

It has been brought to HR's attention that some individuals throughout the company have been using foul language during the course of normal conversation with their coworkers. Due to complaints received from some employees who may be easily offended, this type of language will no longer be tolerated.

We do however, realize the critical importance of being able to accurately express your feelings when communicating with coworkers. Therefore, a list of TRY SAYING new phrases has been provided so that proper exchange of ideas and information can continue in an effective manner without risk of offending our more sensitive employees.

INSTEAD OF: When the fuck do you expect me to do this?
TRY SAYING: Perhaps I can work late.

INSTEAD OF: No fucking way.
TRY SAYING: I'm certain that is not feasible.

INSTEAD OF: You've got to be shitting me.
TRY SAYING: Really?

INSTEAD OF: Tell someone who gives a shit.
TRY SAYING: Perhaps you should check with . . . .

INSTEAD OF: It's not my fucking problem.
TRY SAYING: I wasn't involved in that project.

INSTEAD OF: What the fuck?!?!
TRY SAYING: That's interesting.

DFEH-0018

INSTEAD OF: Fuck it, it won't work.
TRY SAYING: I'm not sure I can implement this.

INSTEAD OF: Why the hell didn't you tell me sooner?
TRY SAYING: I'll try to schedule that.

INSTEAD OF: Who the fuck cares?
TRY SAYING: Are you sure this is a problem?

INSTEAD OF: He's got his head up his ass.
TRY SAYING: He's not familiar with the problem.

INSTEAD OF: Kiss my ass.
TRY SAYING: So you weren't happy with it?

INSTEAD OF: Fuck it, I'm on salary.
TRY SAYING: I'm a bit overloaded at this moment.

INSTEAD OF: Shove it up your ass.
TRY SAYING: I don't think you understand.

INSTEAD OF: This job sucks.
TRY SAYING: I love a challenge.

INSTEAD OF: Who the hell died and made you boss?
TRY SAYING: You want me to take care of that?

INSTEAD OF: Another fucking meeting!!!!
TRY SAYING: Yes, we really should discuss it.

INSTEAD OF: I really don't give a shit.
TRY SAYING: I don't think this will be a problem.

INSTEAD OF: He's a fucking prick.
TRY SAYING: He's somewhat insensitive.

INSTEAD OF: She's a ball busting bitch.
TRY SAYING: She's an aggressive go getter.

INSTEAD OF: You don't know what the fuck you're doing.
TRY SAYING: I think you could use more training.

——————————————-End forwarded Message——————————————————

DFEH-0019

From: sschmit@PacQuad.com

To: jwalsh, sfrigate, jlynch, jradville, arowe, lmorrisey

Sent: 2/3/YR-1

Subject: Enjoy

——————————————————-Forward Header——————————————————-

From: G_C_HONICK@BURTONCONSTR.HR.COM

To: sschmit@PacQuad.com, jcollins@aol.com,slink@clestica.com

Sent: 2/3/YR-1

Subject: Note from Human Resources

————————————————-Forwarded Message———————————————————

What is the difference between a permanent secretary and a temporary secretary?

A permanent secretary screws ON the desk.

———————————————-End forwarded Message——————————————————

DFEH-0020

Jean Long
220-3 Bercado Place
Nita City, Nita

Cold fish :(Glasses Over qualified

EXPERIENCE

YR-10–Present **Manager, Medical Staff Office, Nita Hospital, Nita City, Nita**

Managed a division of Quality Assurance which included: physician credentialing and hospital utilization analysis; preparation of cash flow statements to determine the feasibility of capital equipment purchases; supervised one support staff person; conceived idea to computerize credentialing and utilization review components onto dBase and Lotus 1-2-3 software; implementation is expected to decrease operating expenses by 50 percent within second year.

YR-12–YR-10 **Assistant to Senior Vice President, External Resources, Nita Hospital, Nita City, Nita**

Assisted V.P. in raising money for capital equipment campaigns for not-for-profit hospital; analyzed economic data and prepared fund raising proposals; analyzed and responded to inquiries regarding memorial gifts, securities donations, and private trust fund contributions. Given additional responsibility to solicit donations from corporate and special prospect donors.

YR-15–YR-12 **Freelance Medical Editor/Research Analyst, Nita University Medical Center, Nita City, Nita**

Edited manuscripts published in surgical and anesthesia journals; researched and wrote first draft of medical history book. Research included library work, telephone and personal interviews, and Freedom of Information Act correspondence.

YR-18–YR-15 **Budget Analyst, Nita University Health Policy Institute, Nita City, Nita**

Conducted in-depth computer and manual analysis of consultant expense reports for federally funded grant of $8 million; made recommendations and implemented reimbursement policies which resulted in decreased consultant fees and travel expenses.

YR-20–YR-19 **Legal Assistant, Miller & Miller, Nita City, Nita**

Performed legal research for medical malpractice defense attorneys; drafted legal documents.

Pass

PQ-0007

EDUCATION

YR-13 **Nita University**

Bachelor of Science Degree, Mass Communications with concentration in Political Science; Deans List; Academic Scholarship Recipient

PERSONAL INTERESTS

Skiing, travel, theater, swimming, sailing, and rafting

References furnished upon request.

PQ-0008

Nina Forgo
642 Vista Drive
Nita City, Nita

Not friendly
Bleached hair
Too snobby

Job Objective:

To demonstrate competency in many areas of office work, including word processing.

Skills:

- Typing: 67 wpm
- Shorthand: 70 wpm
- Data Entry: 62 wpm

PC Training:

- Word
- Excel
- WordPerfect

Office Machines:

- Calculator
- Copy Machine
- Microfile
- Records Management
- Adding Machine
- Machine Transcription
- Telephone Training

Communicating Skills

- Proofreading
- Legal Transcription
- Filing
- Accounting I

Education:

- AS Degree, Secretarial: Legal Option, Nita University
- Recognized with honors for school and community involvement. Graduated YR-7.
- Diploma. Nita High School, Nita City
- Majored in business. Graduated YR-9.

Work Experience:

- Nita City International Corporation, Nita City, Nita
May YR-8–August YR-3. Summer Replacement.

Duties: Secretarial. Typing, Filing, Data Input, Mail Sorting and Distribution, Answered and Handled Telephone Calls.

Pass

PQ-0009

• Nita Photography, Inc., Nita City, Nita
August YR-10–August YR-9.

Duties: Filing, Data Entry, Answered and Handled Telephone Calls, Prepared Final Orders for Customer Pick-Up, Scheduled Appointments, Prepared Props to be used in Photographs.

• Nita Department Stores, Nita City, Nita
September YR-11–August YR-10.

Duties: Customer Assistance, Cash Register Operator, Till Drawer Operator, Stocking and Cleaning.

Personal:

• Special Awards: Academic Achievement in Office Machines and Computing I & II. Business Professionals of America First Place State Winner: Office Assistant YR-7.

• Member: Business Professionals of America Chapter Officer YR-8 to YR-7. Student Senate YR-8 to YR-7. Nita University Drug Task Force YR-7.

• Traits: Dedicated, Professional, Organized, Confidential, Responsible, Dependable, Non-Smoker, Friendly Disposition, Well-Spoken, Punctual and Tactful.

References:

Available upon request.

PQ-0010

Sue Robinson
1127 Kinyon Street
Nita City, Nita

Bow Wow
Mack will owe me!

Career Objectives	To work with people who are professional and dedicated to the company's goals.	
Abilities	Book keeping, typing, dictation, filing, copying, telephone skills. Good communicator.	
	Software:	Microsoft Word, Microsoft PowerPoint, Excel, Lotus 123
Education	Nita East High School - business preparatory program	
	Courses:	typing, dictation, book keeping, business law, people skills
	Activities:	Junior Business League, Chess club, Daily Announcements, Orchestra (viola)
Experience	Sid's Stereo Shack - sales representative March YR-1 to present Top Seller - July YR-1	
	Moss & Caldwell Construction - secretary and receptionist August YR-2 to March YR-1	
	Juice Barn - Food preparation specialist Evenings and weekends YR-4 to June YR-2	

Hired

PQ-0011

Alice Rowe

1040 Redwood Lane Nita City, Nita
(721) 555-1047

Experience with computer cos cute – Body!!

Work Experience

* Leviathan Computers, 2600 Industrial Way, Nita City, Nita.
Program Assistant
January–August YR-2.

* Starbuck Software, 5301 Wharf Boulevard, Nita City, Nita.
Administrative Assistant
January–August YR-3.

* Nita Marine Insurance Company, 100 Ring Road, Nita City, Nita.
Administrative Assistant
September YR-5–July YR-4.

* GAM Software, 53 53rd Street, Nita City, Nita.
Administrative Assistant
January–August YR-5.

Skills

* Proficient in Microsoft Office applications, Apple applications, Adobe Acrobat PDF, Photoshop, graphic web design, LINXUS,OS/2.

Education

* Nita State University, Nita City, Nita. Completed 105 of 120 units required for BS in Computer Science. Grade point average 3.5.

* Central High School, Nita City, Nita. Diploma awarded, YR-10. National Honor Society.

Hired

PQ-0012

RESUME

Sharp ✓
Redhead
Very friendly

Caroline Kirk
2235 Pierre Drive
Nita City, Nita

EMPLOYMENT HISTORY

** Clerical; Nita Temporary Staffing Services, Nita City, Nita YR-3 to Present.

– Duties included accounts payable, data entry, purchase orders, shipping/ receiving, typing, filing, telephone, reception.

** Sales Representative; Nita City Fan Company, Nita City, Nita; January YR-4 to December YR-4.

– Initiated new commercial accounts, including the search for new prospects. Was responsible for preparing and costing proposals.

Was responsible for servicing and following-up on accounts.

** Business Sales Representative; Nita Mutual Insurance Co., Nita City, Nita YR-5 to YR-4.

– Initiated new commercial accounts, including the search for new prospects. Was responsible for reviewing and renewing current policyholder accounts. Worked closely with support department, i.e. Underwriting, Claims, and Loss Prevention.

VOLUNTEER

** Appointed School Board Member - Nita Avenue Preschool.

** Classroom aide at Nita Avenue Preschool.

** Girl Scouts of America.

** Sunday School Teacher.

EDUCATION

** Nita University, Nita City, Nita, BS Psychology, YR-6

Hired

PQ-0013

LIZ MORRISEY
P.O. Box 442
Nita City, Nita

She can edit my documents! Petite-cute, bouncy Short hair

QUALIFICATIONS PROFILE

AA - Office Administration - Martha White Business College
Administrative/technical skills
Editing/writing experience
Background in purchasing, inventory control, scheduling
Extensive computer experience/desktop publishing
Teaching/curriculum

EMPLOYMENT HISTORY

Miles, Inc. - Information Specialist - Sept. YR-7 – present; Correspondence/documents using WordPerfect, Microsoft Word for Windows, and Lotus; database management, technical reports, property accounting, purchasing/receiving, and inventory control.

Nita City Department of Public Education - School publications editor - desktop publishing, correspondence, grants Oct. YR-10 – Sept. YR-7

Nita City Department of Public Education - Teacher - School Year YR-9/10

CONTRIBUTION/SKILLS

Editor, Nita Army National Guard Newsletter, Nita

Book Reviewer, VOYA Magazine

Hired

PQ-0014

CINDY LEONARD

Wow
Great Credentials
Long Brown Hair

WORK EXPERIENCE

Project Analysis, Inc.
Research Assistant: YR-3 – Present

Conducted statistical analysis, research, and management for capital projects involving environmental restoration projects, production and manufacturing processes, and process upgrades. Areas of responsibility include study and survey of Engineering Function Centralization system development and training, Capital Reinvestment, Bio-remediation, European and SUPERFUND Environmental Cleanups, presentation development. Clients include Department of Energy and Environmental Protection Agency. Professional Development: "Total Quality Management," "Team Building," "Environmental Legislation."

Market Opinions, Inc.
Intern: August YR-4 – December YR-4

Assisted market research for presidential, congressional, and gubernatorial campaigns. Projects focused on survey design, research, database management, candidate and media correspondence. I also coordinated the video library.

University of Nita Library
Student Aide: September YR-4 – November YR-4

Assisted students with periodical collections and research trials.

EDUCATION

University of Nita
Bachelor of the Arts in Political Science YR-4

Minor: Statistics - Institute for Social Research; Inter-University Consortium for Political and Social Research. Studies: regression analysis, design of experiments, linear equations, pathway analysis.

SKILLS

Extensive computer experience in IBM/PC, MacIntosh, Mainframe (VM/CMS) and LAN environments. Proficiency in a variety of software packages for statistical analysis, database management, graphics, word processing and spreadsheet analysis.

REFERENCES

Available upon request.

Hired ★

PQ-0015

Opal Jennings
1907 Creekwood Drive
Nita City, Nita

OBJECTIVE: To obtain a position that employs my office administration experiences, and requires abilities in judgment, organization, and communication.

WORK EXPERIENCE:

A real firecracker! Sense of humor

INDUSTRIAL DIELECTRICS, INC., Nita City, Nita
January YR-10 – Dec YR-2

- Position: Assistant to Credit/EDI Manager
  - Develop customer credit and collection programs
  - Monitor past due accounts receivables
  - Coordinate bank deposits
  - Install electronic document interchange (EDI) communication systems
    « Maintain EDI software upgrades
  - Worked with programmer to upgrade date processing systems
    « Computer literacy: BM System i, Windows XP, Excel, Word

– call Ray Watson about this Chic

BUNZL DISTRIBUTION, USA, Nita City, Nita
July YR-13 – June YR-12

- Position: Purchasing Agent, Louisville, KY, Jan YR-12
  - Direct branch office material procurement process
  - Maintain inventory control systems (paper products, sundry, and medical supplies)
    « Responsible for Accounts Payable
- Position: Assistant Buyer/Buyer, Nita City, Nita Mar YR-13
  - Procure paper products for distribution process
  - Coordinate vendor quotation process; correspond with vendors
    « Approve Accounts Payable

BLOCKS DEPARTMENT STORE, Nita City, Nita
Jul YR-16 – Mar YR-13

- Position: Sales Associate
  - Responsible for customer sales and service
  - Monitor inventories

MELVIN SIMON & ASSOCIATES, Nita City, Nita
Jun YR-18 – Nov YR-17

- Position: Accounts Payable Clerk
  - Process invoices for shopping malls

Hired

PQ-0016

EDUCATION

Courses toward Bachelor of Science in Business Education
Office Administration
Nita State University September YR-14 to May YR-13

Advanced Training & Seminars:
- Fundamentals of Data Processing Course
- Windows XP Seminars
- Excel Course

PQ-0017

❀ Christine Kolbus ❀
8909 East Webster Pike
Nita City, Nita

Job objectives:	To work in a professional environment gaining business skills to help me reach my life expectations.
Skills:	Typing - 65 wpm; dictation 50 wpm; telephone answering
Business Machines: PBX	IBM & Apple Computers, Dictaphone; Adding Machine;
Experience:	Clothing Barn - Sales Associate Christmas Season YR-5, YR-4, and YR-3
Education:	Nita Central High School Graduated YR-3 (Drama Club, Young American's Achievement Club, Pep Squad, Prom Queen YR-3) Nita Community College (Presently attending night classes toward an AA degree) Program in Business Instruction

This one has the legs to stay
Big eyes

Hired

PQ-0018

JOYCE RADVILLE

1427 Baker Street
Nita City, Nita

EXPERIENCE

NITA STEEL SERVICE, INC. – SECRETARY – AUGUST YR–17 – APRIL YR–3

In the position I held at Nita Steel, I performed many different tasks including such things as: Computerized Order Entry, Invoicing, Inventory Receipts, Adjustments and Transformations, Payroll, Taxes, Approving and Processing Vouchers and Cash Disbursement, Daily Bank Reports, Insurance and Workers' Compensation, General Ledger, and Answering Phones and Greeting Customers and Visitors.

ROSELAND PHARMACY – SALES CLERK – MAY YR–19 – AUGUST YR–17

Being a sales clerk at the pharmacy includes tasks such as: Taking Care of Sales at the Cash, Register, Helping Stock Shelves, and Working in the Postal Substation.

EDUCATION

I attended Nita Technical College where I took Accounting, Business Law, Communications, Credit/Finance, and Computer Programming.

I graduated from Nita High School where I took many business classes including: Typing, Accounting, and Intensive Office Training.

REFERENCES

Available upon request.

Sharp!
Blond
Green eyes

Hired

PQ-0019

PACIFIC QUAD, INC.
A NEW WAVE IN COMPUTERS 24 Beach Avenue Nita City, Nita 99998 (721) 555-5530

June 18, YR-1

Ms. Annie Cunningham
Department of Fair Employment & Housing
30 Van Ness Avenue
Nita City, Nita 99990

Dear Ms. Cunningham:

Please find attached a statement from Ms. Susan Robinson regarding the Alice Rowe case. I do hope that we may resolve this matter soon. If I can be of further assistance, please do not hesitate to let me know. Thank you for your attention.

Sincerely,

John Walsh

John Walsh

President

JW:sr

Attachment

DFEH-0021

I, Susan Robinson, declare:

I am currently employed as a secretary at Pacific Quad, Inc. I have lived in Nita City all my life and have been employed as a secretary in a variety of offices and businesses. During my years as a secretary, I have worked for many executives and have had to work closely with many of them. I can attest to the good character of my current supervisor, Stanley Schmit. Mr. Schmit has always treated me with the greatest respect and courtesy. He has always acted in a highly professional manner and is a model of gentlemanly behavior. I am somewhat shocked to learn of this false accusation against Mr. Schmit. In all the years that I have known Mr. Schmit, I have never seen him conduct himself in any way that would even remotely suggest sexual harassment. I am sure Mr. Schmit will be vindicated in this matter.

Executed on June 18, YR-1 at Nita City, Nita.

I declare under penalty of perjury that the foregoing is true and correct.

Susan Robinson

Susan Robinson

DFEH-0022

DEPARTMENT OF FAIR EMPLOYMENT AND HOUSING

30 Van Ness Avenue   Nita City, Nita 99990

Sept. 10, YR-1

Alice Rowe
1040 Redwood Lane
Nita City, Nita 99998

re: FEP 03-02 A0-OOOse

Dear Ms. Rowe:

Your complaint of discrimination (identified above) is on file with our office. According to the law, the Department must notify you of your right to file a private lawsuit in a Nita Superior, Municipal, or Justice Court on your own behalf. This letter is your notification of that right.

No action is required by you unless you decide to file a private lawsuit. If you choose to exercise this option you must:

1) Notify the Department in writing of your intent; and

2) Provide your own legal counsel; and

3) File your case within one year from the date of this letter.

The Department will continue to process your complaint unless you advise them otherwise. If you do not wish to file a civil suit under Nita law, you need not respond to this letter.

Sincerely,

Mark Alber

District Administrator

cc: Henry Glenn

DFEH-0023

NITA STATE UNIVERSITY

WOMEN'S CENTER

ANNA MILLS, L.C.S.W.

July 22, YR-1

Saul:

Thank you for agreeing to be on call for my clients while I will be away in New York. I did want to alert you about one of my patients, Alice Rowe, whom I have been seeing for about three years. Alice is a single, twenty-six-year-old woman who came to me for career counseling and relational difficulties.

Currently, Alice has one more year of college before graduation but has repeatedly dropped out of school to take part-time secretarial jobs because of a fear of success and lack of self-esteem. Through counseling we have traced much of Alice's self-defeating attitude to her parental relationship. Alice has a hypercritical father and a passive mother. She grew up feeling inadequate, non-assertive, and withdrawn. In addition to her academic and career problems, she has had a continuing conflict with her own femininity.

Although counseling was often difficult, Alice had been making considerable progress and she had a genuine feeling of optimism about the future. She was feeling strong enough to go back to school full-time in September YR-3, to finish her degree in computer science. There was marked improvement in her self-motivation and sense of independence.

However, in February of this year, Alice suffered a significant setback because of a reported incident of sexual harassment at a new job. She was seriously debilitated by the perceived harassment and has been unable to work ever since. She has suffered from insomnia and nightmares. Through increased and intensive counseling, she has made a partial recovery, to the point where she may be ready to go back to work soon. Since the possibility of another misunderstood encounter with a man is very real, I wanted to alert you to Alice's condition. I have discussed your availability with her, and she will be calling on you if she feels the need for counseling or discussion.

Thanks again. I hope all this won't be too much trouble for you.

Anna

Anna

PQ-0020

Law Office
Inter-Office Memorandum

TO: Partner

FROM: Associate

SUBJECT: Rowe v. Pacific Quad - Memo of Law

Per your request, attached is the decision from the Court of Appeals. As you may recall, Pacific Quad was successful in its Motion to Dismiss for failure to state a claim upon which relief can be granted but the Court of Appeals reversed the decision, requiring the parties to move forward with discovery.

IN THE COURT OF APPEALS OF THE STATE OF NITA FIRST DISTRICT

DIVISION 6

ALICE ROWE,	)	
	)	
Appellant and Plaintiff,	)	
	)	
v.	)	Civ. No. 0-09876543
	)	
PACIFIC QUAD, INC.,	)	OPINION
	)	
Respondent and Defendant,	)	
	)	

Argued and Submitted December 15, YR -1

Decided December 30, YR -1

BEFORE: Duba, Presiding Justice, and

Hamater and Pierson, Associate Justices

HAMATER, Justice.

This case comes to this court upon an appeal from a final judgment of dismissal in favor of the defendant in the Superior Court of the County of Darrow after granting the defendant's motion to dismiss for failure to state a claim and granting a motion to strike the prayers for compensatory and punitive damages. For the reasons set forth herein, we reverse.

I. FACTS.

Appellant Alice Rowe brought suit in the Superior Court of Darrow County alleging that respondent, Pacific Quad, Inc., discriminated against her in violation of Nita Government Code section 12940.

Rowe filed a complaint with the Department of Fair Employment and Housing on March 23, YR-1. After its investigation of the complaint but before the Department had made a determination whether to prosecute, Rowe decided to withdraw her complaint and file a civil action. Pursuant to Nita Government Code section 12965, Rowe filed her action in the Superior Court, County of Darrow, on September 20, YR-1. On October 5, YR-1, defendant filed a motion to dismiss for failure to state a claim and moved to strike the prayers for compensatory and punitive damages. By an Order dated October 15, YR-1, the Superior Court, Nolan, J., sustained the motion to dismiss with leave to amend and granted the motion to strike. Rowe did not amend her complaint and a final judgment of dismissal was entered on November 15, YR-1. Rowe then brought this appeal.

In determining whether the motion to dismiss was properly sustained by the Superior Court, this Court must assume the facts alleged in the complaint to be true. *Tameny v. Atlantic Richfield Co.*, 27 Nita 3d 167 (1980); *Strauss v. A.L. Randall Co., Inc.*, 144 Nita App. 3d 514 (2d Dist. 1983).

Briefly summarized, Rowe alleges that she began employment at Pacific Quad in the position of administrative assistant on February 1, YR-2. She further alleges that beginning that day and throughout the week, her immediate supervisor, Operations Manager Stanley Schmit, subjected her to repeated verbal sexual abuse and on February 12, YR-1, made an unsolicited and unwanted sexual advance toward her. She also alleges that both Schmit and Pacific Quad President John Walsh conditioned her continued employment upon her consenting to Schmit's sexual demands. Finally, Rowe alleges that she was constructively terminated in retaliation for her refusal to consent to Schmit's sexual advances.

II. SEXUAL HARASSMENT VIOLATIVE OF THE FAIR EMPLOYMENT AND HOUSING ACT.

The facts alleged, if proven at trial, would require a legal finding of unlawful discrimination in the terms and conditions of employment under the Fair Employment and Housing Act (hereinafter "FEHA"). Nita Gov't Code § 12940(a); see also Nita Admin. Code, tit. 2, §§ 7287.6(b), 7291.1(f)(1).

There are no published decisions of the Nita Courts directly analyzing sexual harassment as a violation of the Nita FEHA. However, the Nita FEHA was modeled after the California FEHA and Title VII of the 1964 Civil Rights Act, which have spawned a number of precedents from the California and federal courts. These decisions provide a detailed analysis of sexual harassment under the California FEHA and Title VII, and provide us with helpful guidance in determining our own standard. Thus, the following analysis draws extensively on California law as well as federal law.

In *Lyle v. Warner Brothers*, 132 P.3d 211, 219 (Cal. 2006), the California Supreme Court held:

> With certain exceptions not implicated here, the FEHA makes it an unlawful employment practice for an employer, "because of the . . . sex . . . of any person, . . . to discriminate against the person in compensation or in terms, conditions, or privileges of employment." (§ 12940, subd. (a).) Likewise, it is an unlawful employment practice for an employer, "because of . . . sex, . . . to harass an employee." (§ 12940, subd. (j)(1).) Under the statutory scheme, "'harassment' because of sex" includes sexual harassment and gender harassment. (§ 12940, subd. (j)(4)(C).) These prohibitions represent a fundamental public policy decision regarding "the need to protect and safeguard the right

> and opportunity of all persons to seek and hold employment free from discrimination." (*Brown v. Superior Court* (1984) 37 Cal. 3d 477, 485, 208 Cal. Rptr. 724, 691 P.2d 272; see also *Mogilefsky v. Superior Court* (1993) 20 Cal. App. 4th 1409, 1414, 26 Cal. Rptr. 2d 116.)

That Court continued, citing its own earlier decisions: "'the prohibition against sexual harassment includes protection from a broad range of conduct, ranging from expressly or impliedly conditioning employment benefits on submission to or tolerance of unwelcome sexual advances, to the creation of a work environment that is hostile or abusive on the basis of sex.'" *Id.* at 219 (quoting *Miller v. Dep't of Corr.*, 115 P.3d 77 (Cal. 2005)).

The Lyle Court further held that under the California FEHA and

> Title VII, a hostile work environment sexual harassment claim requires a plaintiff employee to show she was subjected to sexual advances, conduct, or comments that were (1) unwelcome (see *Meritor, supra*, 477 U.S. at 68); (2) because of sex (*Oncale v. Sundowner Offshore Services, Inc.* (1998) 523 U.S. 75, 80–81, 118 S.Ct. 998, 140 L.Ed.2d 201 (Oncale)); and (3) sufficiently severe or pervasive to alter the conditions of her employment and create an abusive work environment (*id.* at p. 81; *Meritor, supra*, 477 U.S. at 67). In addition, she must establish the offending conduct was imputable to her employer. (*Meritor, supra*, 477 U.S. at 69–73) California courts have adopted the same standard for hostile work environment sexual harassment claims under the FEHA. (See, e.g., *Fisher v. San Pedro Peninsula Hospital* (1989) 214 Cal. App. 3d 590, 608, 262 Cal. Rptr. 842.)
>
> *Lyle*, 132 P.3d at 220.

A. Sexual Harassment.

Sexual harassment is defined by the Nita Code as "verbal, physical, and visual harassment, and unwanted sexual advances." Nita Admin. Code, tit. 2, § 7291.1(f)(1), 7287.6(b). Verbal harassment, as defined by the Nita Code, includes "epithets, derogatory comments, or slurs." Nita Admin. Code, tit. 2, § 7287(b)(1).

Pacific Quad asserts that Rowe's claims cannot meet this definition. The key phrase in the Nita FEHA for determining sexual harassment is that there must be "unwanted sexual conduct." Each word of this phrase represents a distinct test. First, a plaintiff must prove that the alleged *conduct* actually occurred. Second, the plaintiff must prove, by a subjective standard, that the conduct was *unwanted.* Third, the trier of fact must determine whether a reasonable person would interpret the words or actions of the defendant, in light of all the surrounding circumstances, to be sexual.

We find that the facts alleged, if true, meet this definition of sexual harassment.

B. Adversely Affected Employment Benefit.

If sexual harassment did occur, the next issue is whether the sexual harassment affects the complainant adversely by depriving her of an employment benefit. *See* Nita Admin. Code, tit. 2, § 7286.5(f). There are three employment benefits that may be adversely affected.

1. Termination.

An employer terminates an employee when continued employment is conditioned upon accession to sexual demands. Nita Admin. Code, tit. 2, § 7287.6(b)(1)(D). The condition can be express or implied. Here, plaintiff alleges that such a condition was implied when John Walsh told her to leave if she was not happy with the job. Thus, Alice Rowe states facts that would support a finding of termination, a clearly adverse action.

2. Constructive Termination.

Victims of sexual harassment may be forced to quit jobs they otherwise enjoy because they are no longer able to tolerate the offending behavior. Constructive termination occurs where the working conditions are so intolerable that the employee could not be reasonably expected to have remained at her job.

Here, plaintiff/appellant alleges that she was forced to resign because of Stanley Schmit's sexual harassment and the non-responsiveness of John Walsh to take any corrective action. This, too, if proven, constitutes an adverse action.

3. Hostile Work Environment.

Even when there are no conditions placed upon the employee that lead to a termination or constructive termination, the employer may still be liable for a violation of the FEHA if the sexual harassment created a hostile work environment. A discrimination-free workplace or a work environment free of sexual harassment is itself an employment benefit that may not be adversely affected by an employer.

As the California Supreme Court explained in *Miller v. Department of Corrections*, 115 P.3d 77, 87–88 (Cal. 2005):

> According to the Fair Employment and Housing Commission (FEHC), the agency charged with administering the FEHA, harassment on any basis prohibited by the FEHA includes (but is not limited to) verbal harassment, including "epithets, derogatory comments or slurs on a basis enumerated in the Act"; physical harassment, including "assault, impeding or blocking movement, or any physical interference with normal work or movement, when directed at an individual on a basis enumerated in the Act"; and visual harassment, including "derogatory posters, cartoons, or drawings on a basis enumerated in the Act." (Cal. Code Regs., tit. 2, § 7287.6, subd. (b)(1)(A), (B) & (C).) The regulations also specify that "unwanted sexual advances which condition an employment benefit upon an exchange of sexual favors" constitute harassment. (*Id.*, § 7287.6, subd. (b)(1)(D).) In the specific context of sexual discrimination, prohibited harassment may include "verbal, physical, and visual harassment, as well as unwanted sexual advances." (*Id.*, § 7291.1 subd. (f)(1).)
>
> Past California decisions have established that the prohibition against sexual harassment includes protection from a broad range of conduct, ranging from expressly or impliedly conditioning employment benefits on submission to or tolerance of unwelcome sexual advances, to the creation of a work environment that is hostile or abusive on the basis of sex. (*Fisher v. San Pedro Peninsula Hospital* (1989) 214 Cal. App. 3d 590,607–608, 262 Cal. Rptr. 842; see also *Mogilefsky v. Superior Court* (1993) 20 Cal.

> App. 4th 1409, 1414–1415, 26 Cal. Rptr. 2d 116.). . . . We have agreed with the United States Supreme Court that, to prevail, an employee claiming harassment based upon a hostile work environment must demonstrate that the conduct complained of was severe enough or sufficiently pervasive to alter
>
> the conditions of employment and create a work environment that qualifies as hostile or abusive to employees because of their sex. (See *Aguilar v. Avis Rent A*
>
> *Car System, Inc., supra*, 21 Cal. 4th at p. 130, 87 Cal. Rptr. 2d 132, 980 P.2d 846, relying upon *Harris v. Forklift Systems, Inc.* (1993) 510 U.S. 17, 21, 114 S.Ct. 367, 126 L.Ed.2d 295.) The working environment must be evaluated in light of the totality of the circumstances: "[W]hether an environment is 'hostile' or 'abusive' can be determined only by looking at all the circumstances. These may include the frequency of the discriminatory conduct; its severity; whether it is physically threatening or humiliating, or a mere offensive utterance; and whether it unreasonably interferes with an employee's work performance." (*Harris v. Forklift Systems, Inc., supra*, 510 U.S. at p. 23, 114 S.Ct. 367.)

The appellant alleges that Schmit subjected her to two weeks of verbal sexual harassment and then made an unsolicited and unwanted sexual advance toward her. Such facts are sufficient to support a finding that plaintiff was subjected to a hostile work environment, which constitutes an adverse action.

C. Employer Liability.

The last element of a cause of action for sexual harassment under the FEHA is that the employer be liable for the sexual harassment. In this regard, there is a difference between Nita law, which follows California law, and federal law under Title VII.

Under California law, which Nita has adopted, an employer is strictly liable under the FEHA for sexual harassment by a supervisor. *See State Department of Health Services v. Superior Court*, 79 P.3d 556 (Cal. 2003). But the avoidable consequences doctrine applies to damage claims under the FEHA, and under that doctrine a plaintiff's recoverable damages do not include those damages that the plaintiff could have avoided with reasonable effort and without undue risk, expense, or humiliation. *Id.*

As the court explained,

> In this particular context, the defense has three elements: (1) the employer took reasonable steps to prevent and correct workplace sexual harassment; (2) the employee unreasonably failed to use the preventive and corrective measures that the employer provided; and (3) reasonable use of the employer's procedures would have prevented at least some of the harm that the employee suffered.
>
> This defense will allow the employer to escape liability for those damages, and only those damages, that the employee more likely than not could have prevented with reasonable effort and without undue risk, expense, or humiliation, by taking advantage of the employer's internal complaint procedures appropriately designed to prevent and eliminate sexual harassment.
>
> *Id.* at 565.

(By contrast, under Title VII, in cases involving sexual harassment not involving a "tangible employment action," such as demotion or termination, an employer may establish a partial or complete defense by proving: "(a) that the employer exercised reasonable care to prevent and correct promptly any sexually harassing behavior, and (b) that the plaintiff employee unreasonably failed to take advantage of any preventive or corrective opportunities provided by the employer or to avoid harm otherwise." *Burlington Industries, Inc. v. Ellerth*, 524 U.S. 742, 765 (1998); *Faragher v. City of Boca Raton*, 524 U.S. 775, 807 (1998).)

Accordingly, we reverse the judgment of dismissal in favor of the defendant Pacific Quad, Inc., and remand the case with instructions to the trial court to vacate its order sustaining the motion to dismiss and enter an order denying it. We now turn to the question of damages raised by the motion to strike. We also reverse the trial court's decision on this motion, and direct the reinstatement of the prayers for compensatory and punitive damages.

III. RELIEF UNDER THE FAIR EMPLOYMENT AND HOUSING ACT FOR UNLAWFUL SEXUAL HARASSMENT.

The respondent, Pacific Quad, Inc., has objected to the plaintiff's request for compensatory and punitive damages. The Nita Supreme Court has held, however, that compensatory and punitive damages are available to remedy violations of the FEHA. *Commodore Homes Systems, Inc. v. Superior Court*, 32 Nita 3d 211 (1982). Respondent asserts that Commodore is distinguishable because it involved race discrimination, which is entitled to greater legal protection. The case cannot be so narrowly read.

Compensatory damages are properly available to compensate the victim of sexual harassment for the intangible, but nonetheless very real, injury suffered in the form of fear, emotional distress, shame, and humiliation.

Exemplary or punitive damages are also available under Nita law where the employer's actions in violation of the FEHA are sufficiently oppressive, fraudulent, or malicious. Nita Civil Code § 3294; *Commodore Homes Systems, Inc. v. Superior Court, supra*. Nita Civil Code section 3294 specifically authorizes punitive damages where there is oppression, fraud, or malice. Malice exists where there is conduct that is intended to vex, injure, harass, or annoy, or that is taken in conscious disregard of the rights or safety of others. Oppression exists where a person is subjected to cruel and unjust hardship in conscious disregard of that person's rights. Nita Civil Code § 3294(c); *Kreiger v. Pacific Gas and Electric Co.*, 119 Nita App. 3d 137, 148 (3d Dist. 1981).

A corporate employer is liable for punitive damages for the acts of oppression, fraud, or malice of an officer, director, or managing agent of the corporation. A corporate employer may also be held liable for punitive damages for the acts of oppression, fraud, or malice of any other employee of the corporation if an officer, director, or managing agent of the corporation ratifies those actions. Nita Civil Code § 3294(b); *Agarwal v. Johnson*, 25 Nita 3d 932, 951 (1979); *Egan v. Mutual of Omaha Insurance Co.*, 24 Nita 3d 809, 822 (1979); *see also DFEH v. Donald Schriver, Inc., supra.*, at 19.

A managing agent is a person who is vested with sufficient authority that he or she is helping to run the company. Some examples of a managing agent's functions are hiring and firing, disciplining employees, and purchasing important items for company use.

A corporation may also be held liable for conduct of other employees if it ratifies such conduct. Ratification may be established by circumstantial or direct evidence demonstrating adoption or approval of the employee's actions by the corporate agent. *Hale v. Farmer's Insurance Exchange*, 42 Nita App. 3d 681, 692 (4th Dist. 1974). Such ratification may be inferred from the fact that the employer, after being informed of the employee's actions, does not fully investigate and fails to repudiate the employee's conduct by redressing the harm done and punishing or discharging the offending employee. *Sandoval v. Southern California Enterprises, Inc.*, 98 Nita App. 2d 240, 250 (2d Dist. 1950); *McChristian v. Popkin*, 75 Nita App. 2d 249, 256–257 (2d Dist. 1946).

Here, the complainant alleges that Schmit is a managing agent and, furthermore, that Walsh, as president of Pacific Quad, Inc., ratified Schmit's conduct. If the appellant can prove either of these allegations and further prove oppression, fraud, or malice, she would be entitled to punitive damages.

Judgment reversed and case remanded to the trial court for further proceedings consistent with this opinion.